Salads

Abbreviations used

cm	centimetre
in	inch
g	gram
kg	kilogram
oz	ounce
lb	pound
ml	millilitre
l	litre
cl	centilitre
fl oz	fluid ounce
pt	pint
qt	quart
tbsp	tablespoon
tsp	teaspoon
P	protein
F	fat
C	carbohydrates

© Naumann & Göbel Verlagsgesellschaft mbH, a subsidiary of
VEMAG Verlags- und Medien Aktiengesellschaft, Cologne
www.apollo-intermedia.de
Complete production: Naumann & Göbel Verlagsgesellschaft mbH, Cologne
Printed in Poland
All rights reserved
ISBN 3-625-11219-1

Salads

NAUMANN & GÖBEL

Contents

Sauces
for Salads

Dressings bring zest to a salad.
Whether they are based on vinegar
and oil or on yoghurt or mayonnaise,
you will find the right sauces
and dressings to complement any
taste on the following pages.

Salad Dressing

1 onion
2–3 tbsp fruit or wine vinegar
3 tbsp sunflower oil
salt
pepper

1 Peel the onion and chopped it finely.

2 Mix the onions with the vinegar and oil, add salt and pepper to taste. Serve with a green leaf salad.

Per serving:
approx. 86 kcal/362 kJ
1 g P • 9 g F • 1 g C

Variation 1

Mix 1 pressed clove of garlic, 2 tbsp of chopped mixed herbs and 1 tsp Dijon mustard together with the base dressing. Serve with a mixed salad.

Per serving: approx. 89 kcal/375 kJ

1 g P • 9 g F • 2 g C

Variation 2

Mix the base dressing with balsamic vinegar and olive oil. Serve with a tomato salad and carpaccio.

Per serving: approx. 86 kcal/363 kJ

1 g P • 9 g F • 2 g C

Variation 3

For this dressing mix 2 tbsp red wine vinegar, 1 tsp lemon juice and 1 tsp sherry and add 1 tbsp of chopped dill. This dressing is for asparagus salads.

Per serving: approx. 90 kcal/379 kJ

1 g P • 9 g F • 2 g C

Variation 4

Mix 3 tbsp white wine vinegar and 4 tbsp chilli oil and stir in 1 or 2 tbsp of freshly chopped coriander. This sauce goes well with vegetable and rice salads.

Per serving: approx. 100 kcal/419 kJ

1 g P • 10 g F • 3 g C

Warm Vinaigrette with Thyme

4 tbsp aceto balsamico
6 tbsp cold pressed olive oil
1 tbsp fresh chopped thyme
1 tbsp fresh chopped rosemary
salt
pepper

Per serving: approx. 162 kcal/681 kJ
0 g P • 18 g F • 0 g C

Put the vinegar, oil, thyme and rosemary in a pan and slowly warm the mixture while stirring with a whisk. When the mixture is warm enough, remove from the heat and add salt and pepper to taste. Serve with a tomato salad.

Sesame and Lime Dressing

3 tbsp sesame (tahini)
juice and peel from 1 or 2 untreated limes
1 pressed clove of garlic
1 pinch of ground red paprika
1 tbsp chopped coriander
salt
black pepper

Per serving: approx. 35 kcal/146 kJ
1 g P • 2 g F • 2 g C

Mix the tahini, lime juice and peel, garlic and ground paprika. Fold in the coriander and add salt and pepper to taste. Serve with an aubergine salad.

Herb Dressing

100 ml (3 fl oz) thistle oil
50 ml (2 fl oz) white wine vinegar
1 tbsp finely chopped parsley
1 tbsp finely chopped chives
1 tbsp finely chopped dill
1 tbsp finely chopped chervil
1 tbsp finely chopped basil
1/4 tsp salt
1/4 tsp pepper
1 pinch Cayenne pepper

Per serving: approx. 229 kcal/964 kJ
0 g P • 25 g F • 1 g C

Mix the oil, vinegar and herbs in a bowl. Add the salt, pepper and cayenne pepper to taste. Let it stand for about 12 hours. Serve with vegetable, noodle, or rice salads.

Basil Dressing

2 cloves of garlic
1 large bunch of basil
1 tbsp white aceto balsamico
6 tbsp olive oil
2 tbsp freshly grated Parmesan
salt
pepper

Per serving: approx. 174 kcal/733 kJ
1 g P • 19 g F • 1 g C

Peel the garlic, wash and pat dry the basil. Then combine the garlic, basil, 1 pinch of salt and aceto balsamico in a mixer. While the mixer is running, slowly pour oil into the mixture until it is well blended. Fill a bowl with the mixture add cheese then add pepper to taste. Serve with a green leaf or vegetable salad.

Sherry Dressing

3 tbsp sherry vinegar
2 tbsp dry sherry
1 tsp herb mustard
1 pinch of sugar
1/4 tsp salt
1 pinch Cayenne pepper
white pepper
5 tbsp grape seed oil

Per serving: approx. 45 kcal/189 kJ
0 g P • 4 g F • 1 g C

Stir together the sherry vinegar, sherry, mustard, sugar, salt and pepper until the sugar has dissolved. Then slowly stir the oil into the mixture bit by bit until it thickens into a creamy sauce. Serve with a green salad.

Yoghurt Dressing

150 g (5 oz) natural yoghurt
3 tbsp sour cream
the juice of 1 lemon
1 tbsp freshly chopped chives
1 tbsp freshly chopped parsley
salt
white pepper
Cayenne pepper
2 tbsp olive oil

Per serving: approx. 106 kcal/445 kJ
2 g P • 10 g F • 3 g C

Mix the yoghurt, sour cream, oil and herbs together. Add salt, pepper and cayenne pepper to taste. Then slowly stir in the oil. Goes best with green leaf salads.

Red Wine Dressing

1 tbsp chopped shallots
200 ml (7 fl oz) red wine
4 tbsp red wine vinegar
1 egg yolk
1 tsp mustard
1/2 tsp salt
black pepper
100 ml (3 fl oz) sunflower oil

Per serving: approx. 280 kcal/1176 kJ
1 g P • 27 g F • 2 g C

Combine the shallots, red wine and red wine vinegar in a pot and let it cook down by half. Then allow it to cool. Add the egg yolk, mustard and spices, then gradually pour in the oil. Stir until the dressing is creamy. Serve with green leaf and vegetable salads.

Lemon Cheese Dressing

1 clove of garlic
2 tbsp lemon juice
1 tsp of grated lemon peel, from a dry untreated lemon
1 tbsp chopped parsley
1 tsp white wine vinegar
1 tbsp grated Gruyère cheese
salt
black pepper
150 ml (5 fl oz) extra virgin olive oil

Per serving: approx. 340 kcal/1428 kJ
0 g P • 37 g F • 1.5 g C

Peel and finely chop the clove of garlic and mix with the other ingredients. Add the olive oil by drops while stirring until the sauce is of a creamy consistency. Serve with noodle salad.

Tomato Dressing

2 dried tomatoes in oil
1 clove of garlic
1 tbsp capers
6 black olives without stones
2 tbsp aceto balsamico
75 ml (2.5 fl oz) extra virgin olive oil
1 pinch sugar
black pepper

Per serving: approx. 255 kcal/1071 kJ
1 g P • 27 g F • 3 g C

Chop up the tomatoes, peeled clove of garlic, capers and olive oil in a mixer. Stir the vinegar and oil mixture into a smooth paste. Add salt and pepper to taste. Serve with green salads or vegetable salads.

Orange Yoghurt Dressing

100 g (3,5 oz) natural yoghurt
100 ml (3 fl oz) cream
juice of 1 orange
salt
black pepper

Per serving: approx. 108 kcal/455 kJ
2 g P • 8 g F • 6 g C

Mix the yoghurt, cream and orange juice together in a bowl. Add salt and pepper to taste. Goes with rice, noodle and green salads.

Horseradish and Anchovies Dressing

175 g (6 oz) mayonnaise
1 tbsp horseradish from the jar
1 tsp finely chopped anchovies
1 tsp grated onion
1 tsp Worcestershire sauce
1/4 tsp Tabasco

Per serving: approx. 335 kcal/1407 kJ

1 g P • 36 g F • 2 g C

Mix the mayonnaise, horseradish, anchovies and onions together well. Add Worcestershire and Tabasco sauce to taste. Goes well with leaf, vegetable and potato salads.

Tarragon and Chervil Dressing

2 tbsp finely chopped tarragon
2 tbsp finely chopped chervil
200 g (7 oz) crème fraîche
2 tbsp Sherry
2 tbsp rosé
salt
black pepper

Per serving: approx. 151 kcal/635 kJ

1 g P • 15 g F • 2 g C

Mix together the herbs, crème fraîche, sherry and wine and add salt and pepper to taste. Let it stand in the refrigerator for 1 hour. Then spice again to taste. Serve with mushroom and noodle salads.

Malt and Rapeseed Oil Dressing

3 tbsp rapeseed oil
1 tbsp lemon juice
1 tbsp tomato purée
1 tbsp malt vinegar
1 tbsp chopped parsley

Per serving: approx. 36 kcal/150 kJ
0 g P • 4 g F • 0 g C

Take the oil, lemon juice, tomato sauce and vinegar and stir them into a smooth sauce. Fold in the parsley. Serve with bean salads.

Walnut and Honey Sauce

6 tbsp walnut oil
3 tbsp white aceto balsamico
1 tsp clear honey
1 tsp Dijon mustard
1 pinch ground ginger
salt
black pepper

Per serving: approx. 142 kcal/596 kJ
0 g P • 15 g F • 2 g C

Mix together the walnut oil, balsamic vinegar, honey and mustard until smooth. Season to taste with ginger, salt and pepper. Serve this dressing with either goat or sheep cheeses.

Green Sauce

50 g (2 oz) mixed herbs
50 g (2 oz) spinach
250 g (9 oz) mayonnaise

Per serving: approx. 477 kcal/2005 kJ
2 g P • 52 g F • 3 g C

Blanch the spinach and herbs in hot water for 30 seconds. Pour off the water, rinse and dry. Finely chop and mix with the mayonnaise. Serve with egg, vegetable, chicken and fish salads.

Caraway Dressing

115 ml (4 fl oz) sour cream
115 g (4 oz) mayonnaise
5 tbsp white wine vinegar
1 tsp mustard
2 tsp ground caraway (cumin)
1 pinch sugar
salt
pepper

Per serving: approx. 255 kcal/1071 kJ
2 g P • 27 g F • 3 g C

Blend together the sour cream, mayonnaise, vinegar, mustard and caraway together. Season to taste with sugar, salt and pepper. Serve with herb and cabbage based salads.

Herb Sauce with Capers

150 g (5 oz) mayonnaise
50 ml (2 fl oz) sour cream
1 tsp Dijon mustard
2 tbsp diced gherkin
2 tbsp chopped capers
2 tbsp chopped parsley
1 tsp chopped tarragon
salt
black pepper

Per serving: approx. 308 kcal/1292 kJ
1 g P • 33 g F • 3 g C

Mix together the mayonnaise, sour cream and mustard, then add the remaining ingredients. Add salt and pepper to taste. Serve with cold meat, egg and fish salads or vegetables.

Tomato Chilli Dressing

50 ml (2 fl oz) vegetable broth
1 tbsp tomato purée
50 ml (2 fl oz) red wine vinegar
50 ml (2 fl oz) olive oil
1/2 tsp chilli powder
1 tbsp fresh lemon juice
1 tbsp chopped coriander

Per serving: approx. 130 kcal/548 kJ
0 g P • 13 g F • 1 g C

Take all of the ingredients except the coriander and mix them together thoroughly. Finally fold in the coriander. Goes great with salads made from beans or noodles.

Ginger Dressing

1 egg yolk
salt
1 tsp finely grated ginger
70 ml (2.5 fl oz) olive oil
70 ml (2.5 fl oz) walnut oil
1 tbsp coarsely chopped spring onion
black pepper

Per serving: approx. 330 kcal/1386 kJ
1 g P • 37 g F • 1 g C

Blend together the ginger and salt in a mixer. While the mixer is running, slowly add the oil and mix until it is smooth. Finally add the spring onions. Add pepper to taste. Serve with chicken, meat and seafood salads.

Lemon Sauce with Mint

4 tbsp crème fraîche
grated peel and the juice of one lemon
1 tbsp finely chopped mint
2 tbsp mayonnaise
3 tbsp natural yoghurt
salt
black pepper

Per serving: approx. 75 kcal/315 kJ
1 g P • 7 g F • 1 g C

Mix all of the ingredients together and add salt and pepper to taste. This sauce goes well with young tender vegetables such as mange tout and baby corn.

Green Salads
&
Salads with
Mushrooms

Colourful Noodle Salad

Serves 4

200 g (7 oz) whole
wheat noodles
600 ml (1 pt 1 fl oz)
vegetable broth
1 thread of saffron
200 g (7 oz) sweet corn
100 g (3.5 oz) frozen
peas
4 red onions
4 tomatoes
2 avocados
2 yellow peppers
12 very nice lettuce
leaves
1 bunch of coriander
1 red chilli
6 tbsp pumpkin seed
oil
2 cloves of garlic
4 tbsp chopped
pumpkin seeds
salt
pepper

Preparation time:
approx. 25 minutes
Per serving:
approx. 1109 kcal/4640 kJ
21 g P • 66 g F • 64 g C

1 Break the noodles into pieces and let them cook afterwards in a vegetable broth that is 200 ml (7 fl oz) water and contains one thread of saffron for 15 minutes.

2 Strain the corn in a colander. Add the corn and the peas about 8 minutes before the end of the cooking time.

3 Peel the onions and cut into thin rings. Wash the tomatoes and cut into round slices. Peel the avocados, halve and remove the stone. Slice lengthways. Wash, halve and remove the seeds from the pepper. Then cut into strips.

4 Strain the noodles. Then place in a bowl with the sliced onions, tomatoes avocados and strips of green pepper. Then mix together.

5 Wash and dry the lettuce. Then lay out on 4 plates. Wash and dry the coriander. Do the same to the chillies, cut lengthways, remove the seeds and chop finely.

6 Mix together the pumpkin seed oil, coriander and chillies. Peel and press the cloves of garlic and add to the oil.

7 Add salt and pepper to taste and serve.

Spinach Salad with Brie, Sesame and Peaches

1 Clean the spinach, remove the stems and wash thoroughly in water. Then cook the spinach in plenty of salt water for 1 minute. Afterwards, pour off the water and plunge the spinach into cold water. Then allow the spinach to drip dry, then lightly squeeze and chop it coarsely. If you are using frozen spinach, follow the instructions on the packet for thawing, then press out the liquid.

2 Dry roast the sesame seeds in a pan on the stove until they release their

aroma. Cut the Brie into cubes. Wash the peaches, halve them and remove the stones. Divide the peach halves into pieces with a knife and squeeze lemon juice over them.

3 Mix the rest of the lemon juice, salt, pepper and nutmeg together. Then add the rapeseed oil to taste. Mix the spinach, cubes of Brie, sesame seeds and sauce together.

Serves 4

500 g (17 oz) fresh spinach leaves, or 450 g (1 lb) frozen
2 tbsp sesame seeds
200 g (7 oz) Brie cheese
2 peaches
3 tbsp lemon juice
8 tbsp rapeseed oil
salt
pepper
nutmeg

Preparation time:
approx. 20 minutes
Per serving:
approx. 400 kcal/1680 kJ
36 g F • 14 g P • 6 g C

Sprout and Mushroom Salad

1 Wash the mushrooms and cut into pieces. Heat the oil in a pan and sauté the mushrooms in it. Cook for approx. 3 minutes with ginger, mustard and aniseed powder.

2 Take the mushrooms out of the pan. Then wash the sprouts and let them drip dry. Wash the radicchio, then dry and cut into strips. Mix both with the mushrooms.

3 Then mix together the apple vinegar, peanut oil, rice wine and soy sauce with the powdered spices. Mix the sauce with the vegetables and serve.

Serves 4

500 g (17 oz) oyster mushrooms
3 tbsp sesame oil
ginger, mustard and aniseed powder
300 g (10 oz) Alfalfa sprouts
300 g (10 oz) radicchio
3 tbsp apple vinegar
5 tbsp peanut oil
3 tbsp sweet rice wine
2 tbsp soy sauce

Preparation time:
approx. 25 minutes
Per serving:
240 kcal/1003 kJ
7 g P • 21 g F • 2 g C

Smoked Duck Breast with Portobello Mushrooms

Serves 4

150 g (5 oz) rucola
4–8 Portobello
mushrooms
1 tsp mustard
2 pinch of honey
2 tbsp sherry vine-
gar
2 tbsp red wine vine-
gar
2 drops orange
essence
4 tbsp walnut oil
4 tbsp peanut oil
1 piece of fresh
ginger root, approx.
1/2 cm (0.2 in)
salt
pepper
200 g (7 oz) smoked
duck breast

1 Clean the rucola, wash and dry. Remove the stems from the leaves. Put the rucola in a bowl. Thoroughly clean the mushrooms. Then cut into thin strips.

2 For the vinaigrette, whip the mustard, honey, vinegar, orange essence and oil. Peel the ginger root and grate it into the vinaigrette. Add salt and pepper to the vinaigrette to taste. Then spread immediately a little dressing on the mushrooms.

3 Mix the rucola with the rest of the vinaigrette, so that all the leaves are moistened by the dressing. Then arrange the rucola on the plate, with the mushrooms placed on top. Top the dish off with the duck breast and serve at room temperature.

Preparation time:
approx. 15 minutes
Per serving:
approx. 130 kcal/545 kJ
11 g P • 9 g F • 1 g C

Mushroom Salad with Quince Vinaigrette

Serves 4

**4 tbsp white wine
vinegar
1 tbsp quince gelee
salt
pepper
5 tbsp cold pressed
rapeseed oil
1 bunch of chives
1 red onion
1 head red oak leaf
lettuce
300 g (10 oz) fresh
boletus mushrooms
2 tbsp butter
4–8 extra thin
slices of ham**

Preparation time:
approx. 15 minutes
Per serving:
approx. 73 kcal/307 kJ
4 g P • 6 g F • 2 g C

1 Stir together the vinegar and quince gelee. Add a little salt and pepper. Beat in 4 tbsp of oil. Wash and dry the chives and dice and add to the mixture.

2 Peel the onions in to thin almost sheer rings. Also add these to the mixture. Then clean the lettuce, dry and tear into small pieces. Arrange on the plate.

3 Clean the mushrooms, clean with a brush and cut into slices. Heat the butter and fry the mushrooms in it for about 5 minutes. Spice with salt and pepper.

4 Take out the mushrooms and arrange them on the plates on the lettuce leaves. Then arrange the ham on top of the salad and brush everything with the vinaigrette.

Romaine Lettuce with a Blue Cheese Sauce

Serves 4

**1 head of romaine
or any green lettuce
200 g (7 oz) carrots
50 g (2 oz) walnuts
50 g (2 oz) blue
cheese
100 g (3.5 oz) sour
cream
2 tbsp nut oil
1 tsp horseradish
salt
pepper
1 tray of cress**

Preparation time:
approx. 20 minutes
Per serving:
approx. 280 kcal/1176 kJ
27 g F • 5 g P • 4 g C

1 Wash and tear the lettuce into bite-size pieces.

2 Peel the carrots and cut into fine strips or shred.

3 Roast the walnuts in a pan without fat until you can smell the aroma. Take the nuts out of the pan. Let them cool, then chop them coarsely.

4 Press out the blue cheese with a spoon, then mix together with the sour cream, the nut oil and horseradish. Add salt and pepper to taste.

5 Arrange the salad ingredients in a bowl and pour the dressing over it. Chop up the cress and spread it over the salad.

Lombardy Mushroom Salad

1 Dust off the sand from the mushrooms with a brush. Then quarter the mushrooms and cut into slices.

2 Halve the large chanterelle mushrooms. Cut the oyster mushrooms into smaller pieces. Then clean and finely chop the chillies.

3 Peel and finely chop the cloves of garlic. Then wash the parsley and cut into strips.

4 Sauté the mushrooms in 8 tbsp of oil. Then add the chillies, garlic and parsley. Season to taste with salt, pepper and lemon juice. Let the sautéed mushrooms stand for approx. 4 minutes.

5 Then wash the rucola, shake it dry and cut off the stems. To make the dressing, take the rest of the olive oil, the vinegar and the honey and mix them together in a bowl. Season the dressing strongly with salt and pepper.

6 Mix the rucola together with the dressing. Then take the mushrooms out of the pan and shake off the excess oil.

7 Arrange the rucola on 4 plates and divide the mushrooms onto the plates.

Serves 4

400 g (14 oz) yellow boletus mushrooms
200 g (7 oz) chanterelles
200 g (7 oz) oyster mushrooms
1 red chilli pepper
1 clove of garlic
1 bunch of parsley
10 tbsp olive oil
salt
pepper from the mill
2 tbsp lemon juice
250 g (9 oz) rucola
2 tbsp balsamic vinegar
1 tbsp wild honey

Preparation time:
approx. 40 minutes
Per serving:
approx. 392 kcal/1383 kJ
6 g P • 26 g F • 14 g C

Tip
To experience the full flavour of the salad, use only fresh mushrooms.

Gourmet Frisée Salad

Serves 4

150 g (5 oz)
chopped walnuts
1 tbsp Dijon mustard
1 tbsp red wine
vinegar
2 tbsp walnut oil
salt
coarsely ground
black pepper
400 g (14 oz) frisée
lettuce
2 pears
250 g (9 oz)
Gorgonzola

Preparation time:
approx. 25 minutes
Per serving:
approx. 609 kcal/2559 kJ
5 g P • 14 g F • 6 g C

1 Dry roast the walnuts in a pan. Then mix together the mustard, red wine vinegar and walnut oil. Add salt and pepper to taste.

2 Then wash and dry the frisée lettuce and tear into bite-sized pieces. Wash and peal the pear. Cut it into halves, remove the core and cut the flesh into cubes.

3 Then cut the Gorgonzola into strips. Mix all the salad ingredients together and arrange on the plates. Serve with the dressing sprinkled on top and with a buttered and herbed baguette.

Wild Herbs with Baby Pansies

1 Wash and dry the wild herbs. Chop coarsely.

2 Wash and dry the spring onions. Chop into small rings.

3 Peel the cloves of garlic and press. Heat the oil in a pan and lightly sauté the garlic with the spring onions. Spice with the salt and sugar. Then add the pine nuts.

4 Take the pansy petals and wash them. Then tear them with your fingers. Add to the wild herbs and mix them together. Then sprinkle with the garlic sauce.

5 Garnish with flower petals and serve.

Serves 4

250 g (9 oz) wild herbs (young nettle, dandelion, sorrel, coltsfoot)
1/4 bunch of basil
1/4 bunch of Italian parsley
1 bunch of spring onions
3 cloves of garlic
6 tbsp oil
salt
sugar
100 g (4 oz) pine nuts
175 g (6 oz) bouquet of fresh chopped pansies for the garnish

Preparation time:
approx. 25 minutes
Per serving:
approx. 454 kcal/1906 kJ
9 g P • 31 g F • 14 g C

Dandelion Salad with Bacon

1 Loosen the dandelion leaves and wash thoroughly. Then shake the water off, peel the onion and chop.

2 Dice the bacon and fry until crispy.

3 Prepare the salad dressing from the oil, vinegar, onion, salt and pepper. Place the dandelion and bacon into a salad bowl. Pour the salad dressing over the salad and serve with a fresh baguette.

Serves 4

500 g (17 oz) young dandelion leaves
3 spring onions
salt
pepper
150 g (5 oz) smoked bacon
1 tbsp oil
3 tbsp white wine vinegar

Preparation time:
15 minutes
(plus braising time)
Per serving:
approx. 160 kcal/673 kJ
10 g P • 7 g F • 14 g C

Mushroom and Tomato Salad

Serves 4

400 g (14 oz)
mushrooms or
Caesar's mushrooms
2–4 firm tomatoes
100 g (3,5 oz) field
lettuce
5–7 stems of fresh
basil
1 tbsp aceto
balsamico
salt
fresh ground
black pepper
2 tbsp pumpkin seed
or walnut oil
10 walnut kernels
cheddar

1 Brush clean the mushrooms and slice finely. Then wash the tomatoes, remove the stems and slice thinly.

2 Then wash the field lettuce and dry with a paper towel. Then arrange the mushrooms, tomatoes and salad decoratively on large plates.

3 Wash the basil and shake dry. Then tear the leaves off the stems and cut into strips. Take some of the leaves and garnish the sides of the plates.

4 Next, mix together the vinegar and a little salt and pepper. Then add the oil and whisk. Spice to taste. Pour the marinade over the vegetables and let it stand for 15 minutes.

5 Coarsely chop the walnuts. Then dry roast in a pan until golden brown and sprinkle them over the salad. Then add the rest of the basil and top with freshly ground pepper.

6 Cut some very thin slices of cheese and place them on the plate just before serving.

Preparation time:
approx. 15 minutes
(plus standing time)
Per serving:
approx. 196 kcal/822 kJ
7 g P • 17 g F • 5 g C

Tip
Caesar's mushrooms
are considered a great
delicacy and are only
eaten raw. Their avail-
ability on the market
is limited. And the
mushroom collectors
who know where
they grow rarely
betray their secret.

Warm Boletus Salad

Serves 4

**500 g (17 oz) boletus
or other wild
mushrooms
1 clove of garlic
1 tbsp extra virgin
olive oil
salt
200 g (7 oz) butter
1 tbsp freshly
chopped parsley**

Preparation time:
approx. 15 minutes
Per serving:
approx. 228 kcal/958 kJ
2 g P • 24 g F • 1 g C

Tip
A simple white
Bordeaux is perfect for
yellow boletus mush-
room salad – not
to mention a Semillon
or Sauvignon, which
also go well as
aperitifs.

1 Heat the oven to 130 °C/265 °F/gas mark 1/2. Clean the mushrooms with a brush and cut a couple of the mushrooms into thin slices. Place them on 4 fire resistant dishes. Then finely chop the remainder of the boletus mushrooms.

2 Peel the garlic and press. Then brown in hot oil for about 1 minute. After that take them out of the oil and place the chopped mushrooms into the oil and stir at a low heat for about 3–4 minutes. Remove from the stove and let them cool.

3 While the mushrooms are still warm, place them into a mixer and finely purée. Then put the mixture back into the

pan. Turn the heat up just a little. Add butter to the mixture gradually. Do not let the sauce boil!

4 Place the plates with the sliced mushrooms into the pre-heated oven until the mushrooms are warm. Add the parsley to the sauce and pour it over the mushrooms and serve.

Spring Field Lettuce

1 Clean the lettuce and let it drip dry. Then peel the shallots and dice finely. After that, take the recently cooked potatoes and mash them with a fork.

2 Wash and shake the herbs dry. Finely chop. Then beat together the mustard, vinegar, oil and 1–2 tbsp of water in a pot. Add the herbs and stir. Add salt and pepper to taste.

3 Bring the sauce to the boil, then mix together with the mashed potatoes according to taste. Mix the remaining warm sauce with the field lettuce and arrange on the plate. This salad goes especially well with pancakes.

Serves 4

500 g (17 oz) field lettuce
2 small shallots
1 large freshly cooked potato
1/2 bunch of salad herbs (e g. parsley, chives, salad burnet, lemon balm)
1–2 tsp hot mustard
2 tbsp vinegar
4–6 tbsp cold pressed rapeseed oil
salt
pepper

Preparation time:
approx. 20 minutes
Per serving:
approx. 105 kcal/442 kJ
4 g P • 6 g F • 9 g C

Quail Egg Salad in Aioli

Serves 4

250 g (9 oz) light mayonnaise
2–3 tbsp milk
1 tbsp lemon juice
1 tbsp lemon peel
2 cloves of garlic
salt
16 quail eggs
400 g (14 oz) radicchio
200 g (7 oz) celery
150 g (5 oz) cashew nuts

Preparation time:
approx. 30 minutes
Per serving:
approx. 447 kcal/1873 kJ
14 g P • 33 g F • 24 g C

1 For the aioli, mix the mayonnaise, milk and lemon juice until smooth. Then fold in the lemon peel.

2 Peel the cloves of garlic and press with the back of a knife together with a little salt. Then stir into the sauce. When finished, place the mixture into a cool place.

3 Hard boil the quail eggs (4–5 minutes), cool with cold water, then peel and cut in half.

4 Clean the radicchio and dry. Tear into bite-sized pieces. Then take the stalks of celery, wash and clean them very well and then slice.

5 Carefully mix the eggs, lettuce and celery together and sprinkle with cashew nuts. Lightly pour the sauce over the salad and serve with ciabatta bread.

Swedish Mushroom Salad

Serves 4

500 g (17 oz) fresh
wild mushrooms
1 bunch of spring
onions
50 g (2 oz) butter
salt
pepper
200 g (7 oz) endive
2 heads of chicory
100 g (3.5 oz) field
lettuce
100 g (4 oz) cherry
tomatoes
5 tbsp raspberry
vinegar
3 tbsp cane sugar
4 tbsp mustard
1 tsp mustard powder
80 ml (2.5 fl oz)
hazelnut oil
1 bunch of parsley

Preparation time:
approx. 35 minutes
Per serving:
approx. 372 kcal/1562 kJ
10 g P • 32 g F • 15 g C

1 Clean the mushrooms and cut into pieces. Then clean the spring onions and cut into rings. Then heat the butter in a pan and sauté both the mushrooms and the spring onions. Spice with salt and pepper.

2 Clean the endive. Remove the core and cut into strips. Then clean the chicory, cut in half and remove the stalk and cut into strips. Next clean the field lettuce and let it dry.

3 Wash and halve the tomatoes. Place the ingredients together in a bowl, sprinkle with the dried-off mushrooms and mix carefully.

4 Mix the vinegar, sugar, mustard, mustard powder and hazelnut oil together. Wash and dry the parsley, then finely chop and mix half of the parsley, into the dressing. Pour the dressing over the salad and garnish with the remaining parsley.

Mushroom Salad with Mayonnaise Dressing

Serves 4

300 g (10 oz) of
mixed fresh mush-
rooms (e.g. boletus
or wild mushrooms)
the juice of 1 lemon
2–4 tbsp walnut oil
1 egg yolk
salt
pepper
1 clove of garlic
100 ml (3 fl oz) cold
pressed olive oil
vinegar
1 bunch of Italian
parsley

Preparation time:
approx. 15 minutes
(plus frying time)
Per serving:
approx. 147 kcal/616 kJ
3 g P • 14 g F • 2 g C

Tip
For this salad, yellow
boletus is a wonderful
choice The smaller they
are the better.

1 Brush the mushrooms until clean. Then cut into fine slices. Pour the lemon juice over the mushrooms.

2 Pour the walnut oil into a pan and heat. Add the mushrooms and let them cook in the oil for about five minutes while stirring constantly. Then remove from the heat and cool.

3 For the mayonnaise, whip together the egg yolk, salt and pepper and the rest of the lemon juice until it is thick and its volume has increased. Then peel the garlic, press and add to the mixture.

4 Next, add the olive oil to the eggs while stirring constantly. Pour it into the mixture so that there is a constant but very thin stream of liquid going into the yolk. Season the mayonnaise with salt and pepper and some vinegar to taste.

5 Wash the parsley and shake dry. Then chop finely. Then fold it into the mayonnaise. Arrange the mushrooms on the plate, evenly distribute the mayonnaise over the salad evenly and serve.

Colourful Mixed Salad

1 Clean the lettuce and remove the outer leaves. Wash the rest and tear it into bite-sized pieces.

2 Clean the zucchini and slice. Then dice the toasted bread.

3 Melt the butter in a pan and sauté the zucchini in it. Then take out the vegetables from the pan and let them cool. Lightly brown the cubes of bread in the rest of the butter.

4 Cut the cheese into strips. Then clean the grapes, halve them and remove the pips. Wash the tomatoes and cut them in half.

5 Mix together the mustard, salt, pepper, vinegar and oil.

6 Combine and toss the zucchini, tomato halves, cheese and grapes in a large bowl. Then sprinkle the salad with dressing and garnish with the freshly made croutons.

Serves 4

250 g (9 oz) frisée lettuce
250 g (9 oz) red oak leaf lettuce
200 g (7 oz) zucchini
100 g (4 oz) whole wheat toast
2 tbsp butter
200 g (7 oz) semi-soft cheese
100 g (3.5 oz) blue grapes
250 g (9 oz) cherry tomatoes
1 tbsp mustard
salt
freshly ground pepper
3 tbsp aceto balsamico
6 tbsp olive oil

Preparation time:
approx. 20 minutes
Per serving:
approx. 461 kcal/1930 kJ
16 g P • 35 g F • 20 g C

Hearty Pear and Bacon Salad

Serves 4

4 lettuce hearts
150 g (5 oz) walnuts
2 Williams pears
6 tbsp pear juice
6 tbsp pineapple juice
3 tbsp oil
1 tsp creamed horseradish
1 tsp coarse mustard
salt
lemon pepper
1 pinch of sugar
5 tbsp double cream
coriander powder
4 slices of bacon

Preparation time:
approx. 20 minutes
Per serving:
approx. 587 kcal/2468 kJ
5 g P • 48 g F • 26 g C

1 Halve the hearts of lettuce, wash and dry. Set aside a few walnuts and coarsely chop the remainder.

2 Peel, halfe and remove the cores of the pears, quarter them and then cut into thin pieces. Arrange the pear slices and the lettuce hearts on a plate. Then sprinkle with the chopped nuts.

3 With 2 tbsp of pear juice and 2 tbsp of pineapple juice mix the oil, horse-radish, mustard and a little salt, pepper and sugar. Sprinkle the marinade over the lettuce hearts and pears.

4 Mix the double cream with the rest of the juice. Add salt, lemon pepper and coriander powder to taste.

5 Fry the bacon in a pan without fat until crispy. Pour the cream sauce over the salad and arrange the bacon and the rest of walnuts on top of the salad.

Peach-Rucola-Salad

Serves 4

500 g (17 oz) mixed
lettuce
100 g (3.5 oz) rucola
150 g (5 oz)
smoked ham
250 g (9 oz) tinned
peaches
6 tbsp olive oil
3 tbsp vinegar
salt
pepper
cashew nuts for
garnishing

Preparation time:
approx. 20 minutes
Per serving:
approx. 274 kcal/1150 kJ
12 g P • 23 g F • 17 g C

1 Wash and dry the lettuce and tear it into bite-sized pieces. Wash and dry the rucola.

2 Cut the ham into long, thin strips. Strain the peaches in a colander and cut into very narrow pieces.

3 Mix the oil with the vinegar and spice with salt and pepper. Put the salad ingredients into a bowl and sprinkle everything with the dressing. Let it stand for about five minutes.

4 Arrange everything on glass plates and serve garnished with the cashew nuts and some herbs.

TIP:
Would you prefer an alternative
salad dressing? Then spice
100 g (3.5 oz) yoghurt generously
with curry powder, salt and pepper,
and also add a little
peach juice.

Mixed Salad with Wine Cap Mushrooms

1 Clean the lettuce and let it drip dry. Tear the leaves into bite-sized pieces. Dip the tomatoes into boiling water, then peel, remove the seeds and dice. Then wash the carrots, peel and shred them finely.

2 Clean the wine cap mushrooms or the boletus with a brush and cut into fine strips. Heat up in a pan with butter and stir until the mushrooms are brown. Take the sheathed woodtuft mushrooms and strain them in a colander. Then mix with the rest of the wine cap mushrooms and put on one side.

3 Wash the peppers, cut them in half and remove the stalk and the seeds. Then peel and finely chop the shallots and garlic. Then mix all of the ingredients together in a bowl.

4 For the dressing, whip together the vinegar, salt, pepper and oil. Add spice to taste. Wash and finely chop the herbs.

5 Take the dressing and half the salad herbs and mix them with the mushrooms and let them stand for about 15 minutes. Arrange the salad, sprinkle with the rest of the herbs and serve.

Serves 4

**1 small head of
iceberg lettuce
4 tomatoes
2 carrots
300 g (10 oz) wine
cap (garden giant),
boletus or sheathed
woodtuft mushrooms
from the jar
30 g (1 oz) butter
1 yellow pepper
1 orange pepper
1 shallot
1 clove of garlic
2 tbsp vinegar
salt
pepper
3–4 tbsp oil
fresh seasonal herbs**

Preparation time:
approx. 20 minutes
(plus standing time)
Per serving:
approx. 170 kcal/715 kJ
5 g P • 13 g F • 8 g C

Vegetable
Salads

Greek Pumpkin Salad

Serves 4

**1 small pumpkin
(approx. 400 g/14 oz)
1 Spanish onion
1 green pepper
1 red pepper
2–4 mild green
pepperonis
2 tomatoes
2 cloves of garlic
5 tbsp olive oil
100 ml (3 fl oz)
vegetable broth
1 tbsp lemon juice
1 tbsp white
wine vinegar
salt
pepper
2 tbsp fresh chopped
Italian parsley
black olives to taste**

Preparation time:
approx. 30 minutes
(plus cooking time)
Per serving:
approx. 237 kcal/993 kJ
3 g P • 20 g • 11 g C

1 Peel the pumpkin and take out the seeds and inner fibres. Then dice the pumpkin meat.

2 Peel and chop the onion, then wash and deseed the peppers and cut into strips.

3 Wash and dry the pepperoni and cut into small rings.

4 Wash and dry the tomatoes, remove the stems and slice. Then peel and finely chop the garlic.

5 Heat 2 tbsp of olive oil and sauté the cubed pumpkin. Then add the vegetable broth and stew for about 5 minutes so that it still has a strong taste. Then let the pumpkin cool

6 Make a dressing from the lemon juice, vinegar, the rest of the olive oil and the spices.

7 Put the pumpkin cubes and the remaining vegetables into a bowl. Add the dressing and sprinkle with parsley and stir. Add black olives to taste. Place the Greek pumpkin salad into individual bowls and serve.

Zucchini Salad with Melon

Serves 4

1 cantaloupe
1/2 zucchini
1 cucumber
juice of 1 lemon
2 mild pickled pep-
peronis
125 g (5 oz) natural
yoghurt
2 tbsp vegetable oil
2 tbsp freshly
chopped herbs (e.g.
dill, lemon balm,
thyme, parsley,
chives)
salt

Preparation time:
approx. 20 minutes
Per serving:
approx. 96 kcal/402 kJ
2 g P • 7 g F • 5 g C

TIP
This refreshing salad is
delicious on a hot sum-
mer day. You can try
many different types of
melon with this recipe.

1 Peel the cantaloupe and remove the seeds. Wash and clean the zucchini, then peel the cucumber and dice both. Then squeeze the juice of one half lemon onto the vegetables. Wash and dry the pepperoni and cut into rings. Mix all the ingredients together.

2 Make a salad dressing from the yoghurt, oil, herbs, salt and the rest of the lemon juice. Then cover the salad with the dressing. Mix well and serve.

Asparagus with Chopped Eggs

1 Peel the asparagus. Bring a large pot of water to the boil and add some salt and sugar.

2 Place the asparagus into the boiling water and cook for approx. 15 minutes. Then hard boil the eggs, cool in cold water, peel and dice.

3 Gently shake off the excess water from the asparagus and divide onto 4 plates. Douse with vinaigrette and place a quarter of the diced eggs onto each plate. Then sprinkle with finely chopped herbs.

Serves 4

1 kg (2 lb 3 oz) asparagus
salt
sugar
3 eggs
4 tbsp vinaigrette
(see page 10)
fresh herbs (e.g. parsley, chives or chervil)

Peparation time:
approx. 35 minutes
Per serving:
approx. 150 kcal/626 kJ
11 g P • 3 g F • 7 g C

Asparagus and Trout

Serves 4

**1 kg (2 lb 3 oz)
green asparagus
1 tsp salt
1 tsp sugar
200 g (7 oz) smoked
trout
3 tbsp lemon juice
4 tbsp walnut oil
pepper
1/2 bunch of dill**

Preparation time:
approx. 35 minutes
(plus standing time)
Per serving:
approx. 117 kcal/491 kJ
16 g P • 3 g F • 7 g C

1 Wash the asparagus, peel the bottom third and cut off the woodlike ends. Then cut the asparagus into pieces and boil in one 1 l (1 qt) of water for about 10 minutes with 1/2 tsp of salt and 1/2 tsp of sugar.

2 Pour the water off the asparagus and strain. Place the asparagus in a bowl and let the asparagus cool.

3 Cut the trout into thin strips. Mix the oil with lemon juice, the rest of the salt and sugar and the pepper.

4 Wash the dill, shake dry and chop finely. Mix the dill with the dressing and pour over the asparagus. Combine asparagus and trout. Let it stand for about 30 minutes and serve.

Salade Niçoise

Serves 4

5 potatoes
20 green bean pods
225 g (8 oz) tuna
fish in oil
15 broad beans
(fava beans)
1 romaine lettuce
10 sardine fillets
in oil
5 baby artichokes
from the jar
2–3 onions cut in rings
8 cubed tomatoes
1 green pepper cut
into strips
1 chopped stick of
celery
1/2 cucumber
chopped into slices
75 g (2.5 oz) black
olives
10 chopped basil
leaves
5 hard-boiled eggs
175 ml (6 fl oz) olive
oil
3–4 tbsp lemon juice
salt
pepper
2 cloves of garlic

Preparation time:
approx. 40 minutes
Per serving:
approx. 623 kcal/2615 kJ
36 g P • 40 g F • 28 g C

1 Wash the potatoes with a brush under water. Boil for 10 minutes. Pour off the water and dry. Then cut into slices.

2 Then clean the green beans and blanch for about 2 minutes in boiling salt water. Cool with cold water and gently shake off the excess water.

3 Strain the tuna and flake it coarsely with a fork.

4 Take the broad beans out of their pods, blanch them for about 1 minute and cool. While still warm, press the beans out of their hull.

5 Wash and tear the lettuce into smaller pieces. Then dry it. Strain the sardines and the artichokes.

6 Take the vegetables and the lettuce and mix them with the olives and basil.

7 Peel and quarter the eggs. Then take the oil, lemon juice and pepper and mix together. Next, press the garlic and stir into the mixture.

8 Finally, take all of the salad ingredients except the eggs and gently mix them together. Serve with the eggs arranged on the side.

Italian Style Vegetables

Serves 4

250 g (9 oz) zucchini
1 red onion
3 tbsp oil
1 tbsp lemon juice
salt
pepper from the mill
paprika powder
10 g (0.5 oz) Italian
herbs
250 g (9 oz) young
carrots
1 tsp vegetable stock
1/2 tsp sugar
2 tbsp raspberry
vinegar
3 tbsp olive oil
2 sprigs tarragon
1 flat bread
50 g (2 oz)
herb butter

Preparation time:
approx. 50 minutes
Per serving:
approx. 515 kcal/2163 kJ
9 g P • 27 g F • 54 g C

1 Wash the zucchini and cut into thin slices. Peel the onion and cut into rings. Heat the oil in the pan and sauté the zucchini and the onion. Squeeze a lemon over the vegetables and spice with salt, pepper and paprika. Then add the spices.

2 Wash the carrots, peel and cut into long thin strips. Stir in 6 tbsp of water with the vegetable stock in a pot. Then add the sugar and vinegar and bring to the boil. Then blanch the carrot strips in the mixture for about 5 minutes.

3 Let the carrots cool, then strain. Mix together the oil and the carrot strips. Clean the tarragon and tear into small pieces. Then spread the herbs evenly over the carrots. Let this mixture stand for about 15 minutes.

4 In the meantime, warm the flat bread, break it into pieces and spread herb butter over it. Then, arrange the vegetables on a plate and serve.

Bean Salad with Romaine Lettuce

Serves 4

250 g (9 oz) white
beans
salt
black pepper
1 bunch of spring
onions
50 g (2 oz) romaine
lettuce
3 tbsp chopped
Italian parsley
juice of 1 lemon
150 ml (5 fl oz) olive
oil
12 black olives

Preparation time:
approx. 1 hour
(plus soaking time)
Per serving:
approx. 428 kcal/1800 kJ
15 g P • 27 g F • 30 g C

1 Let the beans soak overnight in water. On the following day, cook the beans in the same water with a little salt for about 40 minutes at a medium temperature. Do not let the beans break apart. They should remain whole.

2 Strain the beans and save the liquid. Clean the spring onions and dry them, then cut into rings.

3 Wash the romaine lettuce, shake dry and tear the lettuce into large pieces.

4 Combine the beans, spring onions and romaine lettuce in a bowl.

5 Make a dressing by mixing the lemon juice, oil, 5–6 tbsp of the liquid from the beans, salt, pepper and chopped parsley. Then pour it over the salad. Mix everything well and serve warm with fresh bread.

Insalata Caprese

1 Wash the tomatoes and remove the green stems, then slice.

2 Cut the mozzarella into slices and tear the basil leaves into pieces.

3 Arrange the platter so that the tomatoes and mozzarella slices overlay one another in an alternating pattern. Sprinkle with the torn basil leaves.

4 Stir together the lemon juice, salt and pepper. Then whip together with the oil and pour the dressing onto the salad.

Serves 4

700 g (1 lb 8 oz) beef tomatoes
200 g (7 oz) mozzarella
2 bunchs of basil
20 ml (1 fl oz) lemon juice
salt
pepper from the mill
4 tbsp olive oil

Preparation time:
approx. 15 minutes
Per serving:
approx. 187 kcal/787 kJ
2 g P • 15 g F • 7 g C

Fennel Salad with Oranges

1 Wash the fennel. Separate the greens from the bulb, wash and set aside. Then halve the fennel lengthways and chop into fine slices. Clean and finely chop the spring onions and combine them with the chopped fennel.

2 Peel the oranges with a knife so as to remove the white skin. Collect the juice. Cut the orange into fillets and add to the salad ingredients. Wash the mint and let it dry. Finely chop and add to the salad.

3 Whisk the oil with the vinegar, orange juice, salt and pepper. Pour the dressing over the salad. Mix well. Sprinkle with the top greens of the fennel just before serving.

Serves 4

2 small fennel bulbs
2 spring onions
1 orange
4 fresh mint leaves
4 large fleshy black olives
60 ml (2 fl oz) olive oil
1 tbsp red wine vinegar
salt
coarsely ground pepper

Preparation time:
approx. 15 minutes
Per serving:
approx. 132 kcal/555 kJ
3 g P • 10 g F • 8 g C

Pumpkin Salad with Spinach

Serves 4

3 tbsp chopped
pumpkin seeds
200 g (7 oz)
pumpkin meat
175 g (6 oz) fresh
spinach leaves
24 cherry tomatoes
175 g (6 oz)
feta cheese
2 tbsp white
wine vinegar
1–2 tbsp olive oil
salt
fresh ground pepper

Preparation time:
approx. 10 minutes
Per serving:
approx. 225 kcal/944 kJ
11 g P • 17 g F • 7 g C

1 Dry roast the chopped pumpkin seeds in a pan for about 1–2 minutes. When they start to brown and give off a nice aroma, remove from the heat and let them cool.

2 Cube the pumpkin and cook in a pressure cooker so that it still has a strong flavour. Then let it cool. Take the spinach and wash it thoroughly. Shake dry.

3 Wash the tomatoes, halve them and remove the stems. Then take the feta cheese and cut it into cubes.

4 Arrange the spinach leaves on the plate. Place the pumpkin, tomatoes and feta cheese on top of the spinach. Prepare a dressing from vinegar, oil, salt and pepper and pour over the salad. Sprinkle with roasted pumpkin seeds and serve.

Fresh Vegetable Salad with Jalepeño Peppers

Serves 4

1 zucchini
1/2 cucumber
4 red onions
4 tomatoes
2 mild tinned
jalopeñoes
200 g (7 oz) celery
100 g (3.5 oz) canned
sweet corn
1/2 bunch of cress
1/2 bunch of basil
100 g (3.5 oz) yoghurt
250 ml (9 fl oz)
buttermilk
cumin powder
ground cloves
garlic powder

Preparation time:
approx. 20 minutes
Per serving:
approx. 189 kcal/795 kJ
8 g P • 4 g F • 26 g C

1 Clean the zucchini and cut it into slices. Then wash the cucumber and them cut into slices.

2 Peel the onion and cut it into rings. Wash the tomatoes, halve them and cut into slices.

3 Strain the jalepeño peppers in a colander and cut them into pieces.

4 Clean the sticks of celery and cut them into pieces. Strain the corn and mix the two ingredients together.

5 Wash, dry and chop the herbs.

6 Mix together the yoghurt, buttermilk and basil. Season to taste with the cumin, cloves and garlic powder. Then pour the sauce over the vegetables. Garnish with cress and serve.

White Cabbage and Nectarine Salad

Serves 4

1 small cabbage
(approx. 300 g/10 oz)
1 nectarine or peach
1/2 red onion
3 tbsp low-fat salad
cream
2 tbsp freshly
chopped parsley
1 tbsp fruit vinegar
1 1/2 tsp sugar
1 pinch of ground
pepper

Preparation time:
approx. 20 minutes
(plus cooling time)
Per serving:
approx. 335 kcal/1410 kJ
7 g P • 4 g F • 34 g C

1 Wash and dry the cabbage. Cut into strips or grate. Take the nectarines or peaches, peel, remove the core and cut into slices. Peel and finely chop the onions.

2 Mix the cabbage, nectarine slices and chopped onion in a bowl.

3 Then make a cream for the salad out of the low-fat salad cream, parsley and fruit vinegar. Add sugar and pepper to taste. Then mix everything together and let it stand in a cool place for at least 2 hours.

Chicory Salad with Mandarin Honey Dressing

1 Wash the chicory and remove the stem and hard inner core. Then cut the chicory into 2 cm (0.8 in) wide stripes.

2 Peel the grapefruits with a sharp knife so that the white skin is gone. Carefully separate the grapefruit wedges so that they stay whole and mix them in a bowl with the chicory.

3 Squeeze out and catch the juice from the mandarin oranges. Then fold the mandarins into the salad.

4 Mix together the mustard, honey and pepper paste with 70 ml (2.5 fl oz) of mandarin juice. Spice the sauce with salt, Tabasco and Worcestershire sauce to taste. Then pour the sauce over the salad, mix well and serve.

Serves 4

4 heads of chicory (approx. 500 g/ 17 oz)
2 pink grapefruits
175 g (6 oz) canned mandarins
2 tbsp honey
1 tsp mustard
2 tbsp pepper paste
1 tbsp soy sauce
salt
Tabasco sauce
Worcestershire sauce

Preparation time:
approx. 20 minutes
Per serving:
approx.146 kcal/614 kJ
2 g P • 1 g F • 27 g C

Pepper Salad with Tomatoes

1 Warm the oven to 180 °C/355 °F/ gas mark 4. Wash the peppers, halve them and remove the seeds. Place them face down in a baking pan and cook until the skin is dark brown.

2 Then take the peppers out of the oven and let them cool. Then chop the peppers into cubes.

3 Dip the tomatoes into boiling water and remove the stems, skin and seeds. Chop into 2 cm (0.8 in) pieces. Peel and press the clove of garlic.

4 Place the tomatoes and the peppers into a bowl. Make a dressing from the garlic, vinegar, oil, sugar, salt and pepper and pour it over the vegetables.

5 Let the salad stand for 10 minutes. Wash the coriander, shake dry and chop. Sprinkle on top of the salad.

Serves 4

2 green peppers
1 yellow pepper
3 large tomatoes
1 clove of garlic
1 tbsp sherry vinegar
5 tbsp olive oil
1/2 tsp sugar
salt
black pepper
1/2 bunch of coriander

Preparation time:
approx. 45 minutes
(plus cooling time)
Per serving:
approx. 125 kcal/525 kJ
2 g P • 10 g F • 6 g C

Cucumber Salad with Mint

1 Wash and peel the cucumbers and cut into fine slices. Wash the mint and shake the leaves dry. Remove the leaves from the stems and chop finely. Mix the cucumbers and the mint in a bowl.

2 Make a dressing from the vinegar, oil, orange juice, salt, pepper and orange water and pour it over the cucumbers. Mix everything together thoroughly and let it stand.

3 Cut the orange peel into fine strips and drop briefly into boiling water. Garnish the salad with the orange peel just before serving.

Variation

Cucumber Salad with Rhubarb
Peel and cut the rhubarb. Then place it on a plate, sprinkle with sugar and allow it to draw out the juice. Mix the cucumber with the rhubarb slices. Make a dressing from the fruit juice, olive oil and apple vinegar. Spice and serve.

Serves 4

**2 cucumbers
1/2 bunch of mint
1 tbsp white
wine vinegar
4 tbsp thistle oil
1 tbsp orange juice
salt
black pepper
1 tsp orange blos-
som water
orange peel for
garnish**

Preparation time:
approx. 20 minutes
(plus standing time)
Per serving:
approx. 86 kcal/360 kJ
2 g P • 5 g F • 7 g C

Cucumber and Pumpkin Salad

Serves 4

**1 nutmeg pumpkin
(approx. 500 g/17 oz)
1 cucumber
1 pear
1 onion
2–3 tbsp apple vine-
gar
3 tbsp sunflower oil
1/2 tsp sugar
salt
pepper
paprika powder
fresh chopped
parsley for garnish**

Preparation time:
approx. 20 minutes
(plus standing time)
Per serving:
approx. 142 kcal/596 kJ
2 g P • 9 g F • 12 g C

1 Peel the pumpkin, take out the seeds and the fibres. Cut into large pieces and then slice. Then peel and slice the cucumbers.

2 Wash the pears, take out the seeds and cut the flesh into small pieces. Peel the onions and cut into small cubes.

3 Put the vegetables and fruit into a bowl. Then make a sauce from the dressing ingredients and pour over the salad. Let the salad stand for abaout 30 minutes. Sprinkle with parsley and serve.

Greek Vegetable Salad

Serves 4

**1 head of lettuce
1 tomato
1 small cucumber
1 medium sized onion
1 can of white beans
(approx. 375 g/13 oz)
350 g (12 oz) arti-
choke hearts
from the jar
75 g (2.5 oz) feta
cheese
2 cloves of garlic
1 tbsp dried oregano
5 tbsp yoghurt
dressing
(see page 12)**

Preparation time:
approx. 15 minutes
Per serving:
approx. 400 kcal/1674 kJ
20 g P • 8 g F • 74 g C

1 Wash the lettuce, then shake dry.
Then tear into bite-sized pieces.

2 Wash the tomatoes and remove the
stems and dice.

3 Peel the cucumbers and cut into cubes.
Peel the onions and cut into thin rings.

4 Pour the liquid off the beans and artichokes and strain. Crumble the feta
cheese. Peel and finely chop the cloves of
garlic.

5 Mix all of the ingredients in a bowl.
Fold in the oregano and dressing.

6 Decorate with lettuce leaves, arrange
and serve.

Cucumber Salad with Yoghurt Sauce

Serves 4

2 large cucumbers
salt
500 g (17 oz) yoghurt
1 tbsp olive oil
1–2 cloves of garlic
1 tbsp vinegar
1 tsp mint
1 bunch of chopped
fresh dill

Preparation time:
approx. 20 minutes
Per serving:
approx. 184 kcal/736 kJ
5 g P • 15 g F • 7 g C

1 Peel and cube cucumbers. Place the cucumber cubes into a colander and sprinkle with salt so that the resulting liquid can drip out.

2 Add water to the yoghurt and stir. It should not be too thick nor too thin. It should have a creamy consistency.

3 Peel the cloves of garlic and press them with some salt.

4 Put the cucumbers into a bowl with the rest of the ingredients and mix. Garnish with mint and serve.

Bruschetta with Beans

1 Wash the romanesco and separate the hard blossoms and then blanch in lightly salted boiling water for about 3 minutes.

2 Wash the lettuce and tear into bite-sized pieces. Then strain the romanesco and mix with the lettuce and olive oil.

3 Take the bacon bits and place them in a pan without fat. Then strain the beans.

4 Wash the basil, dry and cut into strips. Then mix the beans and basil together with the pieces of bacon.

5 Mix together the romanesco and lettuce and heat for about 2 minutes. Then add pepper and vinegar to taste.

6 Then slice the bread and brush with garlic oil. Then lightly brown in a pan without fat. Serve everything together.

Serves 4

300 g (10 oz) roma-nesco
salt
1 small head of radicchio
2 tbsp olive oil
150 g (5 oz) bacon bits
300 g (10 oz) white beans from the can
1/2 bunch of basil
black pepper
1 tbsp fruit vinegar
1 ciabatta bread
3 tbsp garlic oil

Preparation time:
approx. 20 minutes
Per serving:
approx. 578 kcal/2418 kJ
22 g P • 25 g F • 65 g C

Artichoke Salad

Serves 4

16 mini-artichokes
4 tbsp olive oil
250 ml (9 fl oz)
yeast vegetable
broth
3 heads of chicory
200 g (7 oz) salami
1 yellow pepper
50 g (2 oz) rucola
50 g (2 oz) field lettuce
100 ml (3 fl oz)
cream
100 ml (3 fl oz) sour
cream
4 tbsp kefir
4 tbsp vegetable
broth
1 tbsp walnut oil
salt
pepper
1/2 bunch of chervil
1/2 bunch of
parsley

Preparation time:
approx. 25 minutes
Per serving:
approx. 443 kcal/1861 kJ
20 g P • 30 g F • 15 g C

1 Clean and dry the artichokes. Then heat the olive oil and sauté the artichokes. Then pour the broth over everything and let it cook on low heat for about 20 minutes. Drain the liquid from the artichokes and allow them to cool. After that, cut off the stalks and cut out the artichoke flesh and slice into pieces.

2 Clean the chicory and cut into pieces. Slice the salami. Wash the pepper, cut it in half, remove the seeds and cut into strips. Then wash and dry the rucola and field lettuce.

3 Mix the artichoke pieces, chicory, salami, rucola and field lettuce in a bowl.

4 Mix together the cream, sour cream, kefir, vegetable broth and the walnut oil. Add salt and pepper to taste.

5 Wash, dry and finely chop the herbs. Then fold them into the mixture. Mix the vegetables with the sauce, arrange on plates and serve.

Zucchini Salad

Serves 4

1 large clove of
garlic
4 tbsp oil
400 g (14 oz) sliced
zucchini
50 g (2 oz) raisins
50 g (2 oz) pine nuts
3 sardine fillets in oil
salt
pepper
3 tbsp mint leaves
2 tbsp lemon juice
small bread slices

Preparation time:
approx. 15 minutes
(plus cooling time)
Per serving:
approx. 298 kcal/1250 kJ
12 g E • 17 g F • 24 g C

1 Peel and press the garlic, then brown in oil. Take out the garlic and dab dry. Then, slice the zucchini and add to the hot oil and cook until softened. Take them out of the oil and drain the excess oil from them.

2 Put the zucchini in a bowl and mix with the raisins, pine nuts, sardine fillets, salt and pepper.

3 Wash the mint and shake dry. Finely chop and add to the mixture. Mix everything together with lemon juice. Then cover the salad and store in a cool place for at least 4 hours.

4 Serve this salad on top of sliced bread.

Green Beans with Rice

Serves 4

**500 g (17 oz) green
beans
2 onions
200 g (7 oz) rice
50 ml (2 fl oz) olive oil
salt
20 g (1 oz) butter
paprika powder**

Preparation time:
approx. 20 minutes
(plus cooking time)
Per serving:
approx. 363 kcal/1523 kJ
7 g P • 17 g F • 46 g C

1 Wash the beans and cut into small
pieces, then place them in a pot.

2 Peel and finely dice the onions. Rinse
the rice and strain it of excess water.
Then add the onions and rice to the beans.

3 Add the oil plus 200 ml (7 fl oz) of
water into the pot. Cook everything on
a very low heat. Add salt after about 5 minutes.

4 Melt the butter in a pan and add the
paprika powder. Place the beans and
the rice into a bowl. Pour the paprika butter
over the salad. This dish can be eaten warm
or cold.

Zucchini Salad with Cashew Nuts

1 Clean and slice the zucchini. Add salt and pepper. Heat 3 tbsp of oil in a pan and fry the zucchini in it for a short time. Pour boiling water over the tomatoes, peel them and remove the stems, then dice the flesh.

2 Wash the spring onions and cut them into small rings. Wash the thyme, shake off the excess water and lay a few of the sprigs to the side for use as garnish. With the remainder, tear off the leaves from the stem.

3 Roast the cashew nuts in a pan without fat until they give off a nutty aroma.

Wash the radicchio, shake it dry and lay the leaves on the plates. Lay the zucchini on top of the leaves with the diced tomatoes.

4 Make a dressing out of the onion, thyme and the rest of the olive oil and balsamic vinegar. Add salt and pepper to taste.

5 Pour the dressing on top of the salad and sprinkle the cashew nuts on top. Garnish with the sprigs of thyme and serve. Goes well with garlic baguettes.

Serves 4

**4 zucchinis
(800 g/1 lb 12 oz)
salt
pepper
10 tbsp olive oil
4 tomatoes
2 spring onions
1 bunch of thyme
100 g (3.5 oz) cashew
nuts
1 head of radicchio
4 tbsp aceto
balsamico**

Preparation time:
approx. 30 minutes
Per serving:
approx. 448 kcal/1880 kJ
8 g P • 40 g F • 15 g C

Warm Vegetable Salad

Serves 4

650 g (1lb 7 oz)
paksoi (bak choy,
Chinese cabbage)
salt
4 onions
2 cloves of garlic
4 tbsp sesame oil
200 g (7 oz) palm
hearts from the jar
200 g (7 oz) bamboo
shoots from the can
200 g (7 oz) white
radish (Daikon)
125 ml (4.5 fl oz)
vegetable broth
2 nori leaves
(seaweed)
8 tbsp soy sauce
6 tbsp lemon juice
8 tbsp sweet
rice wine
3 tbsp sesame oil
5 tbsp vegetable
stock
1 tbsp five-spice
powder

Preparation time:
approx. 30 minutes
Per serving:
approx. 261 kcal/1098 kJ
4 g P • 12 g F • 8 g C

1 Wash and dry the paksoi and then cut into strips. Then blanch in salt water for about 3 minutes and let it drip dry.

2 Peel and dice the onions. Peel and press the garlic.

3 Heat the oil in a pan and sauté the onions and garlic. Drain the palm hearts and the bamboo shoots. Cut into pieces and add to the onions.

4 Wash, peel and dice the white radish. Add it to the vegetable broth and mix with the onions.

5 Roast the nori. Then mix together the soy sauce, lemon juice, rice wine sesame oil, vegetable stock and five-spice powder. Then add salt and pepper to taste.

6 Add the paksoi to the onions and warm. Arrange the mixture on the plates and sprinkle the sauce over the salad. Break up the nori leaves and sprinkle these over the salad.

73

Hearty Herb Salad

1 Clean the outer leaves of the cabbage and quarter. Wash and cut out the hard middle. Then cut into fine strips. Peel the onion and cut into rings.

2 Put the vinegar, sugar and onions into a pot, bring to the boil and then add the cabbage. Add salt and pepper to taste. Then mix in the caraway.

3 Dice the bacon and then fry in the heated oil until crispy. Then mix it into the salad.

4 Let the salad stand to draw in the flavours for 30 minutes. Serve with a pretzel.

Serves 4

750 g (1 lb 10 oz)
white cabbage
2 onions
100 ml (3 fl oz) white
wine vinegar
1 tbsp sugar
salt
white pepper
1 tsp caraway
50 g (2 oz) of
streaky bacon
1 tbsp oil

Preparation time:
30 minutes
(plus standing time)
Per serving:
approx. 133 kcal/559 kJ
5 g P • 7 g F • 12 g C

Pumpkin and Zucchini Salad

Serves 4

2–3 vegetable
pumpkins (approx.
800 g/1 lb 12 oz)
4 zucchinis (approx.
600 g/1 lb 5 oz)
1 large onion
100 ml (3 fl oz) olive
oil
6 tbsp freshly
chopped basil
3 tbsp freshly
chopped mint
2 cloves of garlic
salt
fresh ground pepper
3 tsp aceto
balsamico

Preparation time:
approx. 25 minutes
(plus standing time)
Per serving:
approx. 310 kcal/1302 kJ
6 g P • 26 g F • 14 g C

1 Wash the pumpkin, halve and remove the seeds and inner fibres. Do not peel. Cut the pumpkin into slices. Take the zucchini, wash it and cut into 0.5 cm (0.2 in) thick slices. Peel the onion and finely cut in thin rings.

2 Heat 2 tbsp of oil in a pan. Add the pumpkin and zucchini slices and fry to a golden brown. Then add the rest of the olive oil gradually while cooking.

3 Let the cooked vegetables cool down on a platter. Then arrange with the onion rings.

4 Peel and finely chop the garlic. Make a dressing from the garlic, salt, pepper and vinegar. Then stir in the herbs. Pour all of it over the vegetables. Cover the plate with foil and let it stand for about 1 hour.

Chinese Cabbage Salad

Serves 4

150 g (5 oz)
sweet peas
1 Chinese cabbage
(approx. 400 g/14 oz)
1 small raddichio
1 can of sweet corn
(225 g/8 oz)
100 g (3.5 oz) radishes
1 red onion
2–3 tbsp freshly
chopped ginger
4 tbsp fruit vinegar
2 tbsp vegetable oil
1 1/2 tsp chilli oil
1 tsp sugar

Preparation time:
approx. 25 minutes
Per serving:
approx. 86 kcal/360 kJ
2 g P • 6 g F • 8 g C

1 Cook the sweet peas in a little salt water for about 1 minute. Pour off the water and strain. Set them aside and let them cool.

2 Wash the Chinese cabbage and radicchio, shake off the excess water and shred. Strain the sweet corn. Wash and slice the radishes. Peel the onions and cut into rings.

3 Mix the salad ingredients in a bowl with the ginger.

4 Make a dressing from the fruit vinegar, oil and sugar and pour it over the salad.

Beetroot Salad

1 Strain the beetroot in a colander. Then cut into slices. Strain the sweet corn and peas. Mix the beetroot, peas and sweet corn in a bowl. Peel the eggs, halve them and then mash the egg yolks and dice the egg whites. Mix the yolks with the oil and vinegar. Peel and press the clove of garlic.

2 Drain the onions and the capers and add to the sauce. Add lemon juice, salt, pepper and sugar to taste. Wash the parsley, dry and cut into strips. Stir the parsley and crème fraîche together with the rest of the dressing's ingredients. Arrange the salad on the plates with the dressing. Top with the chopped egg.

Serves 4

800 g (1 lb 12 oz) whole beetroot from the jar
300 g (10 oz) canned sweet corn
200 g (7 oz) canned peas
3 hard boiled eggs
100 ml (3 fl oz) walnut oil
4 tbsp sherry vinegar
1 clove of garlic
100 g (3.5 oz) pearl onions
2 tbsp capers
1 tbsp lemon juice
salt
pepper
1 tsp sugar
2 bunches of parsley
100 g (3.5 oz) crème fraîche

Preparation time:
approx. 30 minutes
Per serving:
634 kcal/2662 kJ
8 g P • 10 g F • 6 g C

Balinese Salad

Serves 4

400 g (14 oz)
black beans
salt
2 tsp shrimp paste
1 large red chilli
2 cloves of garlic
1 tsp chilli powder
juice of 1 lemon
2 tsp brown sugar
1 salad cucumber
4 spring onions
2–3 tbsp finely
chopped mint or
basil leaves
250 g (9 oz) coconut
flakes

Preparation time:
approx. 1 hour and 10 minutes
(plus soaking time)
Per serving:
approx. 440 kcal/1848 kJ
8 g P • 41 g F • 12 g C

1 Soak the beans in cold water for 24 hours. Pour off the water and drain. Then put the beans into a pot and cover them with water. They should cook for between 40 and 50 minutes.

2 Five minutes before they are finished cooking add 2 tsp salt. When the beans are done strain in a colander. Then set to the side.

3 Mash up the shrimp paste. Then wash and finely chop the chilli. Peel and finely chop the cloves of garlic and add to the mixture. Pound everything together and mix in a bowl with chilli powder, lemon juice, sugar and salt. Mix and make it spicy according to taste.

4 Wash the cucumber and the spring onions. Cut the cucumber into thin slices and the spring onions into small thin rings.

5 Take the coconut flakes, cucumber slices, spring onions and beans and mix them carefully together with the sauce. Before serving, toss the salad once and sprinkle with herbs.

China Salad

Serves 4

1 clove of garlic
4 spring onions
2 zucchinis (approx.
300 g/10 oz)
250 g (9 oz) pumpkin
1 red pepper
400 g (14 oz) soya
bean sprouts
1 tbsp dark
soy sauce
2 tsp sweet
chilli sauce
2 tbsp dry sherry
1 tbsp brown sugar
1 tbsp white
wine vinegar
salt
pepper
2 tbsp sunflower oil
1 tbsp sesame oil
1–2 tsp sesame
seeds for garnish

Preparation time:
approx. 35 minutes
Per serving:
approx. 285 kcal/1197 kJ
15 g P • 15 g F • 22 g C

1 Peel and press the garlic. Then wash the spring onions and cut into small rings. Then wash the zucchini and cut into sticks. Cut the pumpkin into strips. Clean the pepper, wash and remove the seeds. Then cut them into strips. Wash the bean sprouts and strain.

2 Then mix together the soy sauce, chilli sauce, sherry, sugar, vinegar, salt and pepper. Heat the vegetable oil in a wok.

3 Cook the garlic and the spring onions in the wok for about 1–2 minutes. Add the zucchini, pumpkin and pepper. Stir all together for another 2 minutes. Add the sauce mixture and let everything simmer together.

4 Add the bean sprouts and cook with the other ingredients for about 2 minutes. Mix everything together, so that the sauce is distributed evenly through the vegetables. Sprinkle with the sesame seeds. Serve the salad warm.

Jerusalem Artichoke and Asparagus Plate

Serves 4

800 g (1 lb 12 oz)
Jerusalem artichokes
3 tbsp herb butter
600 g (1 lb 5 oz) green
asparagus
500 ml (17 fl oz) veg-
etable broth
2 shallots
80 ml (2.5 fl oz)
white wine
1 tbsp white wine vine-
gar
150 ml (5 fl oz) mush-
room broth
salt
pepper
1/4 bunch of tar-
ragon
150 g (5 oz) butter
4 egg yolks

Preparation time:
approx. 45 minutes
Per serving:
approx. 467 kcal/1961 kJ
4 g P • 12 g F • 6 g C

1 Wash and peel the Jerusalem artichokes. Then dice. Heat the herb
butter and sauté the Jerusalem artichoke
pieces in it. Add 50 ml (2 fl oz) of water.

2 Wash and peel the asparagus. Cut off
the ends and cut it into pieces that are
approx. 5 cm (2 in) long. Heat the vegetable broth and cook the asparagus in it
for about 10 minutes.

3 Then take it out and strain. Add the
diced Jerusalem artichoke to the hot,
but not boiling vegetable broth. The diced
vegetables should sit in the broth for 10 minutes at a low heat.

4 Peel and dice the shallots. Bring the
wine, vinegar and mushroom broth to
the boil in a pot and let it cook down by
half. Spice the mixture with salt and pepper.
Then wash and dry the tarragon and chop
it finely. Let the broth cool.

5 Stir the herbs into the mixture. Let the
butter melt in a water bath. Then beat
in an egg yolk. Season the mixture with salt
and pepper.

6 Fold the herb broth into the yoke and
butter. Arrange the asparagus and
Jerusalem artichokes on the plate and pour
the sauce evenly over the vegetables.

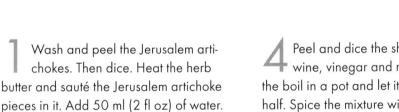

Fennel and Carrot Salad

Serves 4

3 medium sized
fennels
4 carrots
2 tbsp lemon juice
4 slices of multigrain
toast
2 tbsp herb oil
200 g (7 oz) kefir
2 tbsp cream
2 tbsp tomato ketchup
1 tbsp sweet
mustard
100 g (3.5 oz) feta
cheese
salt
pepper
1/2 bunch of basil

Preparation time:
approx. 35 minutes
Per serving:
approx. 379 kcal/1594 kJ
6 g P • 8 g F • 12 g C

1 Wash and grate the fennel, but not too finely. Wash and peel the carrots and also grate them. Mix the fennel and the carrots together and sprinkle with lemon juice. Then cut the toast into cubes.

2 Heat the herb oil in a pan and fry the bread cubes until they are brown and crispy. Then set them on paper towels. For the sauce, mix together the kefir, cream, ketchup and mustard.

3 Crumble the cheese and fold it into the mixture. Spice with salt and pepper. Then wash the basil, dry and cut into strips.

4 Mix the grated vegetables with the sauce and arrange on the plates. Garnish with strips of basil and the croutons, then serve.

Yellow Zucchini Salad

1 Wash the zucchini and cut it into 1.5 cm (0.6 in) thick slices. Then boil with the white wine, vinegar and approx. 500 ml (17 fl oz) of water in a pot. Add sea salt and cook the zucchini slices in it for about 3 minutes while stirring. Remove them from the water and strain.

2 Peel and press the cloves of garlic. Prepare a dressing from the garlic, red wine vinegar, oil, lime peel, mint, oregano and spices. Salt and pepper the dressing heavily.

3 Mix together the zucchini slices and the dressing. Let the salad stand for 30 minutes. Arrange and serve.

Serves 4

**3–4 yellow zucchinis
(750 g/1 lb 10 oz)
125 ml (4 fl oz) dry
white wine
125 ml (4 fl oz) mild
vinegar
1 tbsp sea salt
2 cloves of garlic
2 tbsp red wine vine-
gar
4 tbsp olive oil
grated lime peel
24 small mint leaves
1/2 tsp oregano
salt
fresh ground pepper**

Preparation time:
approx. 45 minutes
(plus cooking and standing time)
Per serving:
approx. 69 kcal/290 kJ
3 g P • 1 g F • 6 g C

Vegetable Salad with Salted Lemons

1 Heat the oven to 180 °C/355 °F/gas mark 4. Wash the peppers, dry and bake in the oven for about 20 minutes, until the skin is black and blistered. Take the peppers out and let them cool. Then peel and remove the seeds and cut into pieces.

2 Wash and dry the aubergines. Then cut into cubes of about 1 cm (0.4 in) size. Separate the eggs and scramble the egg whites. Mix with the vinegar and 1/2 tsp salt.

3 Then cook the aubergines in a pan until it is crispy brown. Take it out of the pan and place it on paper towels.

4 Peel the salted lemon. Wash and dry the lemon peel. Cut the peel into small cubes. Then strain the olives.

5 Mix the pepper, aubergines, lemon peel and olives in a bowl. Make a dressing with the olive oil, lemon juice, salt and pepper. Pour this over the salad. Sprinkle with parsley and serve.

Serves 4

3 green peppers
2 aubergines
2 eggs
1 tbsp fruit vinegar
1 tsp salt
150 ml (5 fl oz) vegetable oil
1/2 of a salted lemon
150 g (5 oz) green olives without stones
2 tbsp olive oil
the juice of 1 lemon
1 tbsp chopped Italian parsley

Preparation time:
approx. 50 minutes
Per serving:
approx. 318 kcal/1334 kJ
8 g P • 29 g F • 10 g C

Salted Lemons

For 10 servings
2 kg (4 lb 6 oz) of untreated lemons
500 g (17 oz) of coarse salt
oil for pouring

Wash the lemons thoroughly. Then cut 5 long cuts into the skin and pack them full of salt. Then put the lemons in a tall heat proof glass and pour boiling water over them. Cover with oil and let them stand for 3 weeks.

Cheese and Brussels Sprout Salad

1 Clean the Brussels sprouts. Cut them in half and cook in salt water for about 5 minutes.

2 In the meantime, mix together the salt, vinegar and pepper. Then mix together with the oil.

3 Peel and finely chop the onion and the clove of garlic. Then stir these into the marinade along with the caraway seed.

4 Wash the parsley and shake it dry. Remove the leaves and chop finely. Then add this to the marinade.

5 Pour off the water from the Brussels sprouts and strain. Mix with the marinade while still warm. Cover and allow to cool.

6 Cut the cheese and the pork sausage into small cubes and mix with the salad. Let it stand for about 10 minutes, then garnish with herbs and serve.

Serves 4

**750 g (1 lb 10 oz)
Brussels sprouts
salt
3 tbsp herb vinegar
freshly ground
pepper
4 tsp grape seed oil
1 onion
1 clove of garlic
1 tsp caraway
1 bunch of parsley
100 g (3.5 oz) pork
sausage
100 g (3.5 oz) gouda
herbs for garnish**

Preparation time:
approx. 20 minutes
Per serving:
approx. 389 kcal/1634 kJ
17 g P • 29 g F • 8 g C

Artichoke Hearts with Peas

Serves 4

2 onions
1 clove of garlic
4 tbsp olive oil
200 g (7 oz) peas
1 jar of pickled arti-
chokes (approx.
280 g/10 oz without
liquid)
2 red peppers
2 thin slices of
Serrano-ham
5 tbsp chopped
parsley
juice from 1/2 lemon
salt
pepper

Preparation time:
approx. 10 minutes
(plus cooking time)
Per serving:
approx. 167 kcal/701 kJ
7 g P • 10 g F • 12 g C

1 Peel the onion and garlic. Cut the onion into thin rings and press the garlic. Heat the oil and add the onions and garlic. Sauté until the onions are glazed, but not brown.

2 Wash and strain the peas. Then strain and halve the artichoke hearts. Then mix the peas and the artichoke hearts with the onion. Cover with water and cook on low heat for about 5 minutes without the lid. Cook until the peas are done, but not a bit more.

3 Cut the peeled and deseeded peppers into strips. Cut the ham into small pieces. Add both to the other vegetables and warm them all together. Then stir in the parsley. Add lemon juice, salt and pepper to taste. Serve lukewarm.

Roman Tomato and Mozzarella Salad

Serves 4

200 g (7 oz) of dried
tomatoes in oil
1/4 bunch of basil
1/4 bunch of
parsley
1 1/2 tbsp capers
1 tbsp balsamic
vinegar
150 ml (5 fl oz) of
the oil from the dried
tomatoes
1 clove of garlic
pepper
100 g (3.5 oz) of
mixed greens
(rucola, spinach,
field lettuce, etc)
500 g (17 oz)
buffalo mozzarella

Preparation time:
approx. 15 minutes
Per serving:
approx. 340 kcal/1428 kJ
25 g P • 25 g F • 3 g C

1 Strain the tomatoes and catch the oil. Then place the tomatoes into a mixer. Wash the herbs. Shake them dry and add them to the mixer. Rinse the capers with water, dry and add them to the mixture.

2 Add the vinegar to the tomato oil and purée everything until smooth. Then peel and press the garlic and mix it with the tomato-herb puree. Spice with pepper to taste.

3 Wash and dry the lettuce leaves and arrange on plates. Cut the mozzarella into slices or cubes and lay these on top of the lettuce. Pour the salad dressing on top and serve.

Papaya Salad
à la Mandalay

1 Peel the papayas, remove the seeds and cut into small pieces. Take the red chilli peppers and crumble them.

2 Wash and dry the Thai-Soi. Then cut into small pieces. Wash the beans, dry and cut into small pieces.

3 Heat the peanut oil and sauté the beans for 5 minutes. Then pour them into a bowl.

4 Then fine purée the papaya and chillies in the mixer. Coarsely chop the cashew nuts and mix with the shrimp paste. Add the lemon juice and stir.

5 Mix together the palm sugar and 3 tbsp of warm water. Then add the mixture to the fish sauce and coconut milk. Wash and cut the tomatoes in half. Then mix everything with the beans. Add papaya paste. Then arrange on plates and serve.

Serves 4

**2 papayas
7 small dried red
chillies
120 g (4 oz) Chinese
chives (Thai-Soi)
50 g (2 oz)
black-eyed peas
3 tbsp peanut oil
2 tbsp unsalted
cashew nuts
1 tsp shrimp paste
3 tbsp lemon juice
1 tbsp chopped palm
sugar
1 tbsp fish sauce
2 tbsp coconut milk
12 cherry tomatoes**

Preparation time:
approx. 20 minutes
Per serving:
approx. 104 kcal/439 kJ
5 g P • 11 g F • 8 g C

Meat, Poultry
&
Fish Salads

Oriental Lamb and Noodle Salad

Serves 4

salt
200 g (7 oz) Turkish
rice noodles
250 g (9 oz) lamb
haunch meat
1 carrot
1 tbsp sunflower oil
black pepper
1 tsp paprika
powder
1 pepper
50 g (2 oz) rucola
3 cloves of garlic
1 bunch of Italian
parsley
3 tbsp lime juice
1 tbsp tahini (sesame
paste)
2 tbsp olive oil
1 lime

Preparation time:
approx. 35 minutes
Per serving:
approx. 320 kcal/1344 kJ
22 g P • 6 g F • 17 g C

1 Boil approx. 3 l (5 pt) of salt water in a large saucepan and cook the rice noodles in it according to the instructions on the packet. Drain and rinse the noodles with cold water.

2 In the meantime, remove the fat and tendons from the meat and dice. Then peel and finely grate the carrots.

3 Heat the sunflower oil in a pan and add the meat. Stir constantly until the meat is thoroughly cooked. Then add the grated carrots and cook for a short while in the oil.

4 Put everything into a bowl and spice with salt, pepper and paprika powder.

5 Wash, halve and remove the seeds from the pepper. Remove the ends and cut the pepper into rings.

6 Clean the rucola, then wash and dry it. Cut into small strips.

7 Peel and press the garlic. Wash, dry and chop the parsley finely.

8 For the dressing, mix the lime juice, the tahini, garlic and olive oil together thoroughly. Then mix in the lamb, the noodles and the other prepared ingredients. Add salt if required.

9 Wash the lime with hot water, dry it and cut into slices. Serve the salad garnished with the slices of lime.

Hamburg Herring Salad

Serves 4

4 raw herring fillets
150 g (5 oz) roast veal
150 g (5 oz) cooked
ham
2 pickled gherkins
150 g (5 oz) of
peeled and grated
beetroot
1 onion
2 apples
4 hard boiled eggs
2 tbsp capers
150 g (5 oz) mayon-
naise
150 g (5 oz) natural
yoghurt
2 tbsp tomato
ketchup
salt
pepper
sugar

Preparation time:
approx. 20 minutes
Per serving:
approx. 625 kcal/2625 kJ
39 g P • 45 g F • 18 g C

1 Soak the herring in water, dry and then chop into large cubes. Chop the roast veal, cooked ham, gherkins and the beetroot into fine cubes.

2 Peel and dice the onions. Wash the apples, cut them in half, remove the cores and cut into small cubes. Then peel and dice the eggs. Drain and coarsely chop the capers.

3 Mix together the mayonnaise, yoghurt and ketchup. Then add salt, pepper and sugar to taste and mix with the salad ingredients. Chill and serve with rye bread and beer.

Gourmet Cold Meat Salad

1 Wash and salt the aubergines. Heat some lemon juice and about 500 ml (17 fl oz) of water in a pot and cook the mini aubergines for about 10 minutes.

2 Wash and slice the cucumbers. Sprinkle with salt. Then take the sausage and cold meat and cut into strips. Peel the shallots and then cut into thin rings.

3 Peel and dice the garlic. Strain the olives and cut them into slices. Strain the aubergines, shake off the excess liquid and cut into slices.

4 Put all of the ingredients into a bowl and mix them. Then stir in the lemon juice and the oil. Wash and dry the herbs and finely chop them. Then add the herbs to the dressing. Spice everything with salt and pepper.

5 Arrange the salad on plates and sprinkle the sauce over it. Garnish the entire dish with the halved quail eggs.

Serves 4

**500 g (17 oz) white and blue mini aubergines
salt
1 cucumber
about 150 g (5 oz) each of three different sausages or cold meats
5 shallots
2 cloves of garlic
50 g (2 oz) green olives without the stones
125 ml (4 fl oz) hazelnut oil
4 tbsp lemon juice
1/2 bunch each of basil, thyme and oregano
pepper
8 quail eggs from the jar**

Preparation time:
approx. 20 minutes
Per serving:
approx. 961 kcal/4024 kJ
32 g P • 82 g F • 14 g C

Gourmet Game Salad

Serves 4

200 ml (7 fl oz) game stock
160 g (5 oz) ready hare back fillets
100 g (3.5 oz) field lettuce
75 g (2.5 oz) chanterelles
150 g (5 oz) brown mushrooms
1 onion
1 tbsp oil
salt
pepper
2 tbsp raspberry vinegar
60 g (2 oz) sour cream
1/2 tsp mustard
1/2 bunch of chives

Preparation time:
approx. 20 minutes
Per serving:
approx. 128 kcal/540 kJ
12 g P • 6 g F • 2 g C

1 Bring the broth to the boil. Take the fillets of rabbit and let them cook at medium heat in the broth for about 10 minutes, then take them out of the broth and let them cool.

2 Wash and dry the lettuce. Wash and slice the mushrooms. Peel and dice the onions.

3 Heat the oil and glaze the onions. Then add the mushrooms and fry them with the onions. Add salt and pepper. Then add 1 tbsp of vinegar and 5 tbsp of the broth. Remove from the heat and let it cool.

4 Cut the meat into thin strips and mix it in with the mushrooms.

5 Divide the lettuce among the plates and place the meat and mushroom mixture on top of the lettuce.

6 Mix together the cream, mustard and the rest of the vinegar, salt and pepper until smooth and pour it over the salad. Sprinkle with chives.

Spicy Liver Salad with Grapes

Serves 4

450 g (1 lb) chicken
or turkey livers
4 tbsp flour
4 tbsp olive oil
salt
pepper
1 bunch of radishes
2 oranges
100 g (3.5 oz) field
lettuce
1 pear
100 g (3.5 oz) seed-
less blue grape
3 tbsp red wine
juice from 1 lemon
5 tbsp grape seed oil

Preparation time:

approx. 25 minutes

Per serving:

approx. 503 kcal/2112 kJ

33 g P • 24 g F • 28 g C

1 Wash and dry the liver, then coat it with flour.

2 Heat the oil in a pan and cook the liver in it. Add salt and pepper.

3 In the meantime, wash the radish and cut it into slices. Then peel the orange completely and remove the fillets. Wash and shake dry the lettuce.

4 Wash the pear, peel and halve. Then take out the seeds and slice. After that wash and halve the grapes.

5 Mix together the red wine, lemon juice and grape seed oil. Add salt and pepper to taste.

6 Arrange the liver, lettuce and fruit on plates. Pour the sauce on top and serve.

Field Lettuce with Chicken Breast and Melon

1 Wash and dry the chicken breast. Then rub it with salt, pepper and paprika powder.

2 Heat 2 tbsp of oil in a pan and cook the chicken breast on each side for about 3 minutes or until it is cooked completely through. Then shake off the excess oil and lay it on paper towels. Let the chicken cool on a plate.

3 Remove the seeds from the cantaloupe. Then scoop out the flesh with an ice cream scoop. Make sure to catch and save all of the extra juice.

4 Take the honey melon, slice open, remove the seeds and also scoop out the flesh.

5 Wash the spring onions and cut them into rings. Then wash and dry the tomatoes and remove the stem and seeds. Cut into eighths. Then wash and dry the field lettuce.

6 Cut the chicken into thin slices.

7 Prepare the dressing, according to taste, from the melon juice, honey, oil and vinegar. Then add salt and pepper to taste.

8 Arrange everything on 4 plates and pour the dressing over the salad.

Serves 4

4 breasts of chicken
mild paprika powder
salt
pepper
4 tbsp vegetable oil
1/2 small
cantaloupe
1 small honey melon
4 spring onions
2 tomatoes
400 g (14 oz) field
lettuce
melon juice
1 tbsp honey
2 tbsp white wine vinegar

Preparation time:
approx. 20 minutes
(plus cooking time)
Per serving:
approx. 293 kcal/1229 kJ
16 g P • 19 g F • 15 g C

Beef Salad

Serves 4

**1 large head
of lettuce
2 tbsp freshly
chopped basil
2 carrots
2 tbsp freshly
chopped parsley
1 yellow pepper
150 g (5 oz) cherry
tomatoes
3 tbsp freshly grated
Parmesan cheese
200 g (7 oz) steak
salt
pepper
75 g (2.5 oz) low fat
natural yoghurt
50 ml (2 fl oz) butter-
milk
3 tbsp finely
chopped onions
3 tbsp mayonnaise
1 tbsp white wine vine-
gar
1 pressed clove
of garlic**

Preparation time:
approx. 35 minutes
Per serving:
approx. 226 kcal/946 kJ
19 g P • 10 g F • 17 g C

1 Wash the lettuce, shake dry and tear it
into pieces.

2 Peel the carrots and cut them into bite-
sized sticks. Wash, dry and dice the
parsley.

3 Clean the pepper and cut it into
cubes. Wash the tomatoes and cut
them in half. Put the vegetables on 4 plates.

4 Cut the beef into strips. Warm a non-
stick pan and add a little oil. Put the
strips of beef into the pan, brown them on
all sides for about 2–3 minutes or until the
flesh is no longer red.

5 Take the pan off the stove. Add salt
and pepper to taste. Then mix in the
basil.

6 Lay the warm beef over the vegetables.

7 Make a dressing from the yoghurt,
buttermilk, Parmesan, onions, mayonnaise, parsley, vinegar, garlic, salt and pepper. Serve with the warm beef salad.

Tip
You can substitute the beef with
low fat chicken or turkey.

Sausage Salad

Serves 4

3 mustard gherkins
from the jar
1 Spanish onion
300 g (10 oz) sausage,
one piece
200 g (7 oz) baby
corn from the jar
1 tbsp vegetable broth
125 ml (4 fl oz)
raspberry vinegar
125 ml (4 fl oz) sun-
flower oil
1 tsp salt
1/2 tsp pepper
1/2 bunch of
parsley

Preparation time:
approx. 40 minutes
Per serving:
approx. 608 kcal/2555 kJ
6 g P • 38 g F • 14 g C

1 Strain the gherkins in a colander and then dice them. Peel and dice the onion. Skin the sausage, first cut it into slices and then into strips.

2 Strain the corn and cut into large pieces. Put it into a bowl with the sausage, onions and gherkins and pour 125 ml (4 fl oz) of boiling water over it.

3 Mix together the vinegar and oil. Add salt and pepper to taste. After the vegetable and sausage broth has cooled add the vinegar and oil. Then, wash and dry the parsley, lay some on the side and cut the rest into strips and fold it into the mixture.

4 Pour the sauce over the ingredients and mix everything together. Then let it stand for about 10 minutes. Arrange everything on plates and garnish with the rest of the parsley.

Potatoes with Smoked Dogfish

1 Wash the potatoes and cook them in their skins. Afterwards, peel them and cut them into thin slices. Then take the mushrooms and brush them clean.

2 Wash and dry the tomatoes and cut them into quarters. Then cut the bacon into fine strips and fry it in 1 tsp of hot olive oil. Heat the broth and pour it over the potatoes.

3 Add the finely cut vegetables and mix everything together. Then spice the salad with vinegar, oil, salt and pepper to taste.

4 Cut the smoked fish into pieces and arrange it with the potato salad. Serve, sprinkled with parsley.

Serves 4

1 kg (2 lb 3 oz) potatoes
1/2 cucumber
125 g (5 oz) celery
250 g (9 oz) mushrooms
4 tomatoes
125 g (5 oz) bacon
olive oil
200 ml (7 fl oz) beef broth
herb vinegar
salt
pepper
3 strips of smoked dogfish or salmon
chopped parsley

Preparation time:
approx. 50 minutes
Per serving:
approx. 435 kcal/1827 kJ
35 g P • 13 g F • 42 g C

Melon with Herring

1 Halve the melon, peel it and remove the seeds with a spoon. Then cut the flesh into pieces.

2 Wash and dry the herring fillets and cut them into bite-sized pieces. Then wash and dry the lettuce and tear it into small pieces. Arrange the melon, herring and lettuce onto plates.

3 Prepare a dressing by mixing the sour cream, lemon juice and spices. Pour this over the salad and serve garnished with dill.

TIP

You can also try this salad with shrimp or North Sea crab instead of herring. For a more refined salad add freshly ground ginger.

Serves 4

**1 cantalope
(approx. 500 g/17 oz)
4 herring fillets
100 g (3.5 oz)
romaine lettuce
50 g (2 oz) sour
cream
juice of 1 lemon
salt
paprika powder
freshly ground
pepper
dill for garnish**

Preparation time:
approx. 15 minutes
Per serving:
approx. 388 kcal/1628 kJ
27 g P • 25 g F • 13 g C

Crayfish Salad

Serves 4

**250 g (9 oz)
romanesco
250 g (9 oz) broccoli
100 g (3.5 oz) green
beans
salt
4 baby pineapples
2 oranges
4 mandarin oranges
150 g (5 oz) celery
1/2 bunch of tar-
ragon
1/2 bunch of dill
125 ml (4 fl oz) olive
oil
4 tbsp lemon juice
400 g (14 oz)
crayfish from the can
pepper
Worcestershire sauce**

Preparation time:
approx. 20 minutes
Per serving:
approx. 505 kcal/2112 kJ
21 g P • 33 g F • 27 g C

1 Wash and cut the blossoms off the romenesco and broccoli. Then wash the beans and cut into pieces. Blanch everything in salt water for about 3 minutes. Pour off the water and strain the vegetables.

2 In the meantime cut off the top of the baby pineapple and hollow out the fruit and cut the flesh into small pieces. Peel the oranges and mandarins, remove the white skin and cut out the individual fillets.

3 Clean and wash the stalks of celery and cut them into pieces. Mix the fruit, celery, romanesco and the broccoli in a bowl.

4 Wash and dry the herbs and chop them finely. Then mix them with the oil and the lemon juice. Cut the crayfish into pieces and mix them into the salad. Season everything with salt, pepper and Worcestershire sauce. Serve the salad in the pineapple shells.

Mussel and Asparagus Salad

Serves 4

800 g (1 lb 12 oz)
green asparagus
salt
sugar
1 tbsp butter
juice of 1 lemon
1 head lollo rosso
2 tbsp lemon juice
1 tbsp herbed mus-
tard
3 tbsp walnut oil
1 bunch of dill
250 g (9 oz) mussels
from a jar
4 pieces of Swedish
marinated salmon

Preparation time:
approx. 50 minutes
Per serving:
approx. 307 kcal/1289 kJ
12 g P • 6 g F • 10 g C

1 Wash the asparagus and cut off the ends.

2 Then take the asparagus and cook them in salt water with a pinch of sugar, butter and lemon juice for approx. 20 minutes.

3 Take the asparagus stalks out and shake off the excess liquid. Then cut them into bite-sized pieces. Then wash the lettuce and cut into wide strips.

4 Mix a dressing from the lemon juice, mustard and walnut oil. Add salt to taste.

5 Wash and dry the dill and then chop it finely. Add it to the dressing. Put the mussels in a colander and strain.

6 Arrange the salad leaves with the asparagus and the mussels on a plate. Then sprinkle the salad with the dressing and serve with the Swedish marinated salmon.

Shrimp and Leek Salad

1 Clean the leeks and cut them into thin rings. Thaw the shrimps, then wash and dry them.

2 Peel the onions and cut into rings. Then cut the bacon into thin strips and fry them in a pan.

3 Mix the crème fraîche with the orange juice and sugar. Add salt and pepper to taste.

4 Pour the sauce over the salad ingredients and sprinkle with chopped nuts.

Serves 4

250 g (9 oz) leeks
250 g (9 oz) shrimps
(frozen)
2 red onions
100 g (3.5 oz)
streaky bacon
200 g (7 oz) crème
fraîche
juice of 1 orange
2 tbsp sugar
salt
pepper
50 g (2 oz) chopped
walnuts

Preparation time:
approx. 25 minutes
Per serving:
approx. 354 kcal/1487 kJ
10 g P • 8 g F • 14 g C

Tip

Leeks in Latin are called "porrum" another common name is "porree". Leeks are the mildest of all the vegetables in the onion family. A salad combining leeks and shrimp make a fruity full bodied salad that supplies the body with special minerals and lifts one's spirits.

Alsace Sausage Salad

Serves 4

2 eggs
400 g (14 oz)
sausage
1 onion
2 tomatoes
4 lettuce leaves
3 tbsp white wine vine-
gar
3 tbsp walnut oil
1 tsp mustard
salt
pepper
2 tbsp freshly
chopped parsley

Preparation time:
15 minutes
(plus cooking time)
Per serving:
approx. 383 kcal/1607 kJ
18 g P • 34 g F • 3 g C

1 Hard boil the eggs for 10 minutes. Take them out of the pot, place them in cold water and let them cool. Cut the Lyoner sausage into slices. Wash and shake dry the lettuce leaves.

2 Wash the tomatoes, remove the stems and cut them into quarters. Then peel and chop the onions.

3 Make a dressing from the vinegar, oil, mustard, salt and pepper.

4 Place the lettuce leaves on the plates. Peel the eggs and cut them in half, then place half an egg on each plate with the tomatoes, chopped onions and sliced sausages topping the leaves.

5 Pour the dressing over the salad and sprinkle with parsley.

Fitness Salad

Serves 4

2 Braeburn apples
(or Pink Lady)
4 carrots
2 papayas
3 tbsp lemon juice
1 bunch of spring
onions
2 heads of chicory
300 g (10 oz) sliced
roast pork
6 tbsp multivitamin
juice
100 ml (3 fl oz)
sour milk
1/2 bunch of parsley
salt
pepper
8 taco shells

Preparation time:
approx. 20 minutes
Per serving:
approx. 314 kcal/1321 kJ
6 g P • 9 g F • 14 g C

1 Peel the apples, halve them and remove the cores. Then grate them. Peel the carrots and grate them also. Then peel the papayas, halve them and remove the stones. Then scoop out the flesh with a spoon.

2 Slice and then dice the papaya. Mix it together in a bowl with the apples and carrots. Sprinkle everything with lemon juice. Then wash and dry the onions and cut into rings.

3 Then wash the chicory and remove the spotted leaves. Then halve it and cut the bitter core into wedges about 4–5 cm (1.5–2 in) thick. Then cut them into narrow strips.

4 Cut the roast pork into strips and mix with the rest of the ingredients. For the dressing mix together the multi-vitamin juice, sour milk, finely chopped parsley, salt and pepper.

5 Pour the dressing over the salad and mix well. Serve in the taco shells.

Pineapple and Chicken Salad

Serves 4

1/4 pineapple
mixed greens
(500 g/17 oz)
1 carrot
4 breasts of chicken
fillets (500 g/17 oz)
some fat for cooking
150 g (5 oz) low fat
pineapple yoghurt
2 tbsp pineapple or
orange juice
1/2 tsp curry powder
1/8 tsp black pepper

Preparation time:
approx. 45 minutes
Per serving:
approx. 221 kcal/925 kJ
25 g P • 4 g F • 21 g C

1 Peel and dice the pineapple.

2 Wash and dry the lettuce, then tear into bite-sized pieces.

3 Wash, peel and coarsely grate the carrots.

4 Wash and dry the chicken breast. Then heat some fat in a non-stick pan and cook the chicken fillets for approx. 5–6 minutes on each side or until they are cooked all the way through.

5 Then add the pineapple pieces to the pan and let them cook for an additional 5 minutes.

6 Divide the salad onto 4 plates. Slice the chicken fillets and lay the slices on top of the pineapple pieces and grated carrots.

7 To make the dressing, combine the yoghurt, pineapple juice, curry powder and pepper. Then pour it on top of the salad.

Spinach Salad with Bacon

1 Wash the spinach thoroughly and shake it dry. Then wash, dry and finely chop the onions.

2 Place the bacon in a non-stick pan and fry until crispy.

3 Heat the vinegar, sugar, salt and pepper in the pan and stir until the sugar is dissolved. Then take the pan off the heat.

4 Mix the spinach and onion with the bacon while it is hot. Keep stirring, for about 1–2 minutes, until the spinach is slightly blanched.

5 Then arrange the salad on the individual plates and serve warm.

Serves 4

250 g (9 oz) fresh spinach
2 spring onions
4 slices of breakfast bacon
4 tbsp white wine vinegar
3 tsp sugar
1/4 tsp salt
1/8 tsp pepper

Preparation time:
approx. 20 minutes
Per serving:
approx. 65 kcal/272 kJ
3 g P • 3 g F • 8 g C

Herring Dip

Serves 4

5 salted herring
400 ml (14 fl oz) milk
100 g (3.5 oz)
mayonnaise
1 Spanish onion
2 pickled gherkins
2 sour apples
salt
pepper
sugar
1 tbsp cranberry sauce

Preparation time:
approx. 25 minutes
(plus soaking and standing time)
Per serving:
approx. 525 kcal/2205 kJ
39 g P • 34 g F • 16 g C

1 Let the salted herring soak in cold water for about 2 hours. Then pour the water off, dry the herrings and remove the bones. After that let the fish soak in milk for 2 hours.

2 Stir the mayonnaise until it is smooth. Then peel and finely grate the onions and mix them into the mayonnaise. Dice the gherkins and mix them into the mayonnaise. Then wash the apples, remove the stem and core and dice finely. Mix it in with the rest of the ingredients and add salt, pepper and sugar to taste.

3 Place the herrings on kitchen towel and let them dry. Then cut the herring and mix with the cranberry sauce and mayonnaise mixture.

4 Let the herrings stand for at least 12 hours before serving.

Lobster Salad with Mint

Serves 4

1 lobster (approx.
1 kg/2 lb 3 oz)
400 g (14 oz) water-
melon
300 g (10 oz) honey-
dew melon
the juice of 1 lemon
2 tbsp acacia honey
6 mint leaves
1 tbsp sugar
3 tbsp grape seed oil
50 g (2 oz) cashew
nuts

Preparation time:
approx. 45 minutes
Per serving:
approx. 547 kcal/2300 kJ
43 g P • 25 g F • 27 g C

1 Put the lobster in boiling water for about 5 minutes. Then break off the shell and the pincers and remove the meat. Then cut the meat into strips.

2 Scoop out the flesh of the melon with an ice cream scoop.

3 Mix together the lemon juice, honey, mint, sugar and oil.

4 Arrange the melon balls decoratively with the lobster meat and pour the sauce over it. Then sprinkle the whole salad with cashew nuts.

Cucumber Salad Royal

Serves 4

4 eggs
1 pinch of tamarind powder
1 small onion
2 cloves of garlic
1 piece of fresh ginger (approx. 2–3 cm/1–1.25 in)
2–3 sprigs of coriander for garnish
1 sprig of lemon grass
1 tsp shrimp paste
1 tsp sugar
1/2 tsp salt
1/2 tsp cumin
1/2 tsp ground pepper
3 1/2 tsp ground turmeric
300 ml (10 fl oz) coconut milk
1 cucumber
shrimps
1/4 bunch of coriander

Preparation time: approx. 40 minutes (plus cooling time)
Per serving: approx. 161 kcal/675 kJ
11 g P • 8 g F • 11 g C

1 Hard boil the eggs. Stir 1 tbsp of water into the tamarind powder and let it stand. Then peel the onion and the cloves of garlic. Then finely chop the onion and add it to the wok. Press the garlic with a knife and add it to the onions in the wok. Peel the ginger, finely chop and add it to the rest.

2 Wash and shake dry the coriander, chop it finely and add it to the wok. Then clean and wash the lemon grass and remove the outside leaves. Cut the light internal stalk into pieces about 1 cm (0.5 in) long and add these to the wok.

3 Mash together the shrimp paste with the sugar, salt, cumin, pepper, tamarind water and turmeric.

4 Mix the turmeric mixture with the rest of the ingredients. Then stir the coconut milk into the mixture and let it boil. Then take it off the stove and let it cool down a bit.

5 Wash the cucumber and cut it into thin slices. Peel the eggs and cut them in half.

6 Arrange the cucumber slices and eggs on a plate. Garnish with the shrimp and coriander leaves. Pour the sauce over the salad and serve.

Caution

It is very difficult to remove turmeric stains from clothing.

Asian Salmon Salad

Serves 4

200 g (7 oz) fennel
bulbs
100 g (3.5 oz)
mange tout
100 g (3.5 oz)
bamboo shoots from
the can or jar
100 g (3.5 oz) palm
hearts from the jar
100 g (3.5 oz) Chi-
nese cabbage
200 g (7 oz)
sour milk
3 tbsp light soy
sauce
3 tbsp rice wine
3 tbsp sesame oil
ginger powder
mustard powder
2 sprigs of
lemon grass
100 g (3.5 oz)
bean sprouts
150 g (5 oz)
smoked salmon

Preparation time:
approx. 25 minutes
Per serving:
approx. 284 kcal/1193 kJ
14 g P • 12 g F • 10 g C

1 Clean, wash and dry the fennel and mange tout. Then cut them into pieces.

2 Shake off the excess liquid from the bamboo shoots and cut them into pieces.

3 Drain the palm hearts in a colander and cut into slices. Clean and wash the Chinese cabbage and cut it into strips.

4 Mix the sour milk with the soy sauce, the rice wine and the sesame oil. Season to taste with the ginger and mustard powder and the finely chopped lemon grass.

5 Rinse the bean sprouts in hot water. Then cut the salmon into strips and arrange on the plates with the vegetables. Pour the sauce over the salad and serve garnished with the bamboo shoots and salmon.

Grapefruit and Prawn Salad

1 Mix together the fish sauce, palm sugar and lemon juice. Then peel and finely chop the cloves of garlic. Clean and wash the spring onions and cut them into rings. Then clean, wash and dry the mange tout.

2 Heat the oil and sauté the garlic, spring onions and mange tout for about 3–5 minutes while stirring. Then take them off the heat and let them cool.

3 Peel the grapefruit and separate the fillets. Wash the watermelon, cut into quarters, remove the seeds and cut the flesh into small pieces. Mix the fruit and prawns together in a large bowl.

4 Wash the red chilli peppers, cut them in half lengthways and then into fine strips. Wash and dry the mint and also cut it into fine strips. Then add both to the salad and pour the dressing over it.

5 Coarsely chop the peanuts and roast them in a pan without fat.

6 Arrange the salad on the plates and serve.

Serves 4

2 tbsp fish sauce
1 tbsp palm sugar
2 tbsp lime juice
2 cloves of garlic
1/2 bunch of spring onions
100 g (3.5 oz) mange tout
1 tbsp sesame oil
1 grapefruit
400 g (14 oz) watermelon
115 g (4 oz) peeled prawns
2 red chilli peppers
1/2 bunch of mint
3 tbsp unsalted peanuts

Preparation time:
approx. 25 minutes
Per serving:
approx. 283 kcal/1191 kJ
12 g P • 12 g F • 14 g C

Shrimp Cocktail

Serves 4

300 g (10 oz) shrimps
1 tbsp lemon juice
150 g (5 oz)
field lettuce
200 g (7 oz) man-
darin oranges from
the can
200 g (7 oz) oyster
mushrooms
100 g (3.5 oz) bean
sprouts from the can
10 tbsp spicy
ketchup
6 tbsp crème fraîche
2 tbsp olive oil
1/2 tsp salt
1/2 tsp pepper
1/2 tsp paprika
powder
4 nice lollo rosso
leaves

Preparation time:
approx. 25 minutes
Per serving:
approx. 316 kcal/1329 kJ
19 g P • 12 g F • 18 g C

1 Rinse and strain the shrimps in a colander. Then put them in a bowl and sprinkle them with the juice.

2 Clean, wash and dry the field lettuce and remove the wilted yellow leaves.

3 Drain the mandarin slices and save the juice.

4 Clean the oyster mushrooms thoroughly, then cut them into pieces. Then strain the bean sprouts.

5 Put the shrimps, mandarin slices, mushrooms and bean sprouts in a bowl and mix them together

6 Mix the ketchup with the crème fraîche, mandarin orange juice, oil, salt, pepper and paprika.

7 Wash and dry the lollo rosso and mix it together with the field lettuce in a glass bowl

8 Put the shrimp cocktail on the plates and pour the sauce over the salad and serve

Tip
Try this refreshing snack with crayfish or king prawns.

Salads with Rice, Noodles & Potatoes

Rice Salad

1 Prepare the rice in a vegetable stock according to the instructions on the packet.

2 Wash and dry the herbs, then chop them finely. Mix the herbs with the olive oil.

3 Strain the black salsifies and the capers in a colander.

4 Then chop the capers finely and mix together with the black salsifies and herbs.

5 Fold in the cream and add salt and pepper to taste.

6 Pour the water off the rice and let it cool. Then combine all of the ingredients and serve.

Serves 4

4 cups of natural rice
1 l (1 qt) vegetable broth
1 bunch of parsley
1 bunch of tarragon
125 ml (4 fl oz) olive oil
300 g (10 oz) black salsifies from the can
1 tbsp capers
150 g (5 oz) sour cream
salt
pepper

Preparation time approx. 20 minutes
Per serving:
approx. 1003 kcal/4201 kJ
17 g P • 38 g F • 45 g C

Multi Colour Pasta Salad

Serves 4

350 g (12 oz)
fettuccini
salt
300 g (10 oz) carrots
40 g (1.5 oz) butter
300 g (10 oz) frozen
peas
6 tbsp vegetable
broth
pepper
1–2 tbsp lemon juice
3 tbsp fruit vinegar
4 tbsp olive oil
1/2 bunch of parsley
200 g (7 oz)
Gorgonzola

Preparation time:
approx. 20 minutes
(plus time for cooling)
Per serving:
approx. 643 kcal/2699 kJ
27 g P • 27 g F • 72 g C

1 Cook the noodles in salt water according to the instructions on the packet until they are firm.

2 Peel the carrots and cut them lengthways into thin strips and then into 2 cm (0.8 in) Melt the butter in a large pan and sauté the carrots at a low heat for 3 minutes. Then add the peas and the vegetable broth to the pan. Cover and let the vegetables cook for 5 minutes. Then add salt, pepper and lemon juice to taste.

3 Pour the water off the noodles and let them cool. In the meantime, make the salad dressing. Take the vinegar and add salt and pepper, then stir in the olive oil. Wash and dry the parsley, then finely chop. Then mix the parsley and vegetables into the salad dressing.

4 Next mix the noodles with the vegetables and the dressing. Break the Gorgonzola into pieces and sprinkle on top of the salad.

Farfalle Salad with Red Lentils

Serves 4

100 g (3.5 oz)
red lentils
500 ml (17 fl oz)
beef stock
300 g (10 oz)
farfalle
salt
1 onion
100 g (3.5 oz) beet-
root from the jar
1 carrot
100 g (3.5 oz) leeks
2 tbsp lemon juice
3 tbsp oil
pepper
2 tsp allspice
powder
1 tsp paprika
powder
150 g (5 oz) smoked
meat
1 bunch of parsley

Preparation time:
approx. 25 minutes
(plus cooling time)
Per serving:
approx. 403 kcal/1690 kJ
21 g P • 7 g F • 63 g C

1 Wash the lentils and cook them in the stock for about 10 minutes on low heat.

2 Cook the noodles in salt water according to the instructions on the packet until they are firm.

3 In the meantime, peel and finely chop the onions. Cut the beetroot into strips. Peel the carrot and cut and chop it into small fine stick-like strips. Then wash the leeks and cut into thin rings.

4 Mix together the lemon juice and the oil. Add salt, pepper, allspice and paprika powder to taste. Cut the smoked meat into strips, then wash, dry and chop the parsley.

5 Strain the lentils and the noodles in a colander. Then let them both cool down completely. Then take the carrots, leeks, onions and smoked meat and mix them with the pasta and lentils. Add the sauce and serve.

124

Tricolour Noodle Salad

1 Wash the aubergine and cut it into slices about 0.5 cm (0.2 in) thick and lay the slices on a plate. Sprinkle with sea salt. Then cover them and place a weight on top and let them stand for about 1 hour. Then rinse them off and dry. Grill the slices for about 4 minutes.

2 Clean the pepper, then wash it, halve it and remove the seeds. Then cut the pepper into strips. Wash the zucchini and cut them in strips. Then cut a cross on the top of each beef tomato. Dip them in boiling water and peel. After that cut them into cubes. Afterwards, strain the cheese in a colander and also cut it into cubes. Finally wash and finely chop the parsley.

3 Cook the noodles according to the instructions on the packet. Then place them in a colander and rinse with cold water. Strain and set the noodles to the side for cooling.

4 Halve the grilled aubergine and mix with the rest of the vegetables and the mozzarella. Season with salt and pepper to taste. Then stir in the parsley and sprinkle with olive oil. Fold in the noodles and serve.

Serves 4

1 large aubergine
4 tsp coarse sea salt
3 red peppers
2 medium sized
zucchinis
2 beef tomatoes
400 g (14 oz)
mozzarella
1/2 bunch of parsley
500 g (17 oz)
coloured tortellini
salt
pepper
125 ml (4 fl oz)
olive oil

Preparation time:
approx. 30 minutes
(plus standing time)
Per serving:
approx. 543 kcal/2278 kJ
47 g P • 24 g F • 33 g C

Chinese Noodle Salad

Serves 4

100 g (3.5 oz) glass
noodles
20 g (1 oz) mu-err
mushrooms
salt
200 g (7 oz)
green beans
1 bunch of spring
onions
1 yellow pepper
2 cloves of garlic
2 tbsp peanut oil
3 tbsp lemon juice
3 tbsp vegetable
stock
1 tbsp sugar
1 pinch of
sambal oelek
parsley for garnish

Preparation time:
approx. 30 minutes
(plus soaking time)
Per serving:
approx. 167 kcal/701 kJ
5 g P • 7 g F • 21 g C

1 Put the glass noodles and the mushrooms in separate bowls. Pour lukewarm water over them and let them soak for about 30 minutes.

2 In the meantime, take about 2 l (2 qt) of salt water and bring it to the boil. Then wash the beans and cut off the tips. Then cut the beans into fine slanted pieces. Briefly blanch the beans in the boiling water, then dip them in cold water and let them dry.

3 Wash the spring onions and cut them into rings. Then clean and wash the yellow pepper, halve it, remove the seeds and dice. Peel the garlic and chop it finely.

4 Strain the noodles and mushrooms. Remove the stems and cut the mushrooms into strips. Cut the noodles into small pieces with kitchen scissors.

5 Heat the oil in a sufficiently large pan and sauté the mushrooms, beans and onions at a low heat while stirring for about 2 minutes. Add the garlic and the red pepper and cook for a short time. Carefully fold in the glass noodles and let everything cook again for a short time. Remove the pan from the heat and let everything cool.

6 While the noodles and vegetables are cooling, mix together the lemon juice, vegetable stock, sugar and sambal oelek. Pour the dressing over the salad and mix everything thoroughly. Maybe add salt to taste.

7 Arrange the noodle salad on a plate or platter, garnish with parsley and serve.

Noodle Salad

Serves 4

**350 g (12 oz)
penne pasta
salt
2 cloves of garlic
500 g (17 oz)
romaine lettuce
100 g (3.5 oz)
Gorgonzola
3 tbsp walnut oil
100 g (3.5 oz)
chopped pecans
8 tbsp kefir
pepper
1 tsp chilli powder**

Preparation time:
approx. 25 minutes
Per serving:
approx. 681 kcal/2853 kJ
20 g P • 36 g F • 68 g C

1 Prepare the noodles according to the instructions on the packet. Then peel and finely chop the cloves of garlic.

2 Wash and dry the lettuce and cut it into strips. Cut the Gorgonzola into cubes.

3 Heat the oil in a pan and sauté the garlic in it. Then add the lettuce and the cheese to the mixture and let it stand for about 3 minutes.

4 Mix together the nuts and the kefir. Then add salt, pepper and chilli powder to taste.

5 Pour the water off the noodles and strain in a colander.

6 Mix the noodles together in a bowl with the ingredients in the pan and serve.

Green Potato Salad

Serves 4

500 g (17 oz)
potatoes
salt
1 bunch of spring
onions
200 g (7 oz)
mange tout
1 green pepper
3 tbsp white wine vine-
gar
freshly ground
pepper
4 tbsp grape seed oil
1 bunch of chervils

Preparation time:
approx. 50 minutes
(plus standing time)
Per serving:
approx. 331 kcal/1391 kJ
5 g P • 18 g F • 30 g C

1 Wash the potatoes and cook them in their skins for about 20 minutes in salt water. Pour off the water, add cold water and let them cool.

2 Wash the spring onions and cut them into small rings. Clean the mange tout and blanch them for about 2 minutes in boiling salt water. Take them out. Rinse them with cold water and let them dry.

3 Clean the pepper, halve it, remove the seeds and the white inner skin. Wash the pepper halves and cut into fine strips. Peel and slice the potatoes.

4 Add salt and pepper to the vinegar and slowly stir the oil into the vinegar drip by drip. Then tear the chervil leaves.

5 Mix together the spring onions, mange tout, pepper strips and chervil leaves and stir in the salad sauce. Let the potato salad stand for about 30 minutes.

Westphalian Potato Salad

1 Clean the potatoes with a brush and water. Then cook them for about 20 minutes. Pour off the water and let them cool a bit. Then peel. Hard boil the eggs, dip them in cold water, then peel the eggs and cut them into slices.

2 Slice the cooled potatoes. Then peel and dice the onions. Wash and peel the cucumber and then cut it into thin slices.

3 Wash, dry and finely chop the chives and the dill.

4 Beat the cream until it is half stiff, then add vinegar, salt, pepper and sugar until it has a strong taste. Mix all of the ingredients into the sauce.

Serves 4

1 kg (2 lb 3 oz) potatoes
3 eggs
3 onions
1 small cucumber
5–6 dill sprigs
1 bunch of chives
250 ml (9 fl oz) cream
vinegar
salt
pepper
sugar

Preparation time:
approx. 50 minutes
Per serving:
approx. 450 kcal/1890 kJ
14 g P • 24 g F • 43 g C

Wild Rice Salad with Apricot

1 Cook the rice according to the instructions on the packet. Afterwards, let it cool for about 10–12 minutes on a platter and stir it occasionally.

2 In the meantime, wash and dry the apple, pepper and celery. Then dice all of these ingredients.

3 Also cut the apricots into cubes. Combine the diced fruit and vegetables in a bowl.

4 For the dressing, mix together the soy sauce, sugar and vinegar in a bowl. Add 2 tbsp of water and stir until the sugar is dissolved.

5 Mix together thoroughly the dressing, rice, fruit and chopped vegetables. Finally, sprinkle peanuts over the salad.

Serves 4

75 g (2.5 oz) mixed
wild rice
1/2 medium sized
apple
1/2 green pepper
1/2 celery
50 g (2 oz) dried
apricots
2 tbsp soy sauce
2 tsp sugar
2 tsp fruit vinegar
25 g (1 oz) unsalted
roasted peanuts

Preparation time:
approx. 35 minutes
Per serving:
approx. 110 kcal/460 kJ
3 g P • 3 g F • 23 g C

Tip
For a flavourful take on this salad
try adding cooked chicken
or turkey breast.

Potato and Fish Salad

Serves 4

**500 g (17 oz) new
potatoes**
salt
**1 bunch of spring
onions**
**150 g (5 oz)
mange tout**
**3 tbsp peppered
butter**
**400 g (14 oz)
mackerel fillet**
**4 tbsp sherry vine-
gar**
3 tbsp red wine
3 tbsp walnut oil
pepper from the mill
1/2 bunch of dill

Preparation time:
approx. 35 minutes
Per serving:
approx. 431 kcal/1812 kJ
12 g P • 14 g F • 18 g C

Tip
The oil in this salad
gives it a very special
resonance. Walnut oil
has a mild nutty taste
and is prized in the
French kitchen. When
combined with sunflower
oil, the sauce acquires
a wonderful culinary
note.

1 Peel the potatoes and cook for 15 minutes in lightly salted water. Wash the
spring onions and cut them into rings.

2 Clean the mange tout. Heat the peppered butter in a pan and sauté the
spring onions and mange tout.

3 Cut the mackerel fillets into pieces.
Then mix together the vinegar, red
wine and walnut oil. Add salt and pepper
to taste.

4 Wash and dry the dill and tear off the
separate leaves. Pour the water off the
potatoes, peel them and cut them into slices.

5 Arrange the vegetables, potatoes and
fish on plates. Pour the sauce over the
salad and garnish with the dill.

Fresh Noodle Salad

Serves 4

250 g (9 oz)
spaghetti
salt
1 tbsp olive oil
100 g (3.5 oz)
cherry tomatoes
1 yellow pepper
150 g (5 oz)
Swiss cheese
4 sticks of celery
100 g (3.5 oz) frozen
Italian herbs
125 ml (4 fl oz)
olive oil
4 tbsp fruit vinegar
(e.g. apple vinegar)
pepper
paprika powder

Preparation time:
approx. 35 minutes
Per serving:
approx. 631 kcal/2651 kJ
8 g P • 6 g F • 14 g C

1 Cook the noodles according to the directions on the packet in lightly salted water for about 10 minutes. Add oil to the water so that the noodles do not stick together.

2 While the pasta is cooking, wash and halve the tomatoes and cut them into thin slices. Wash the pepper and halve it lengthways. Remove the seeds and cut into strips. Then cut the cheese into strips.

3 At the end of the cooking time, rinse the noodles in a colander. Set them to the side and let them cool.

4 Wash the sticks of celery and cut them into pieces.

5 Mix the noodles and the vegetables in a bowl. Mix the thawed herbs together with the oil and fruit vinegar. Then add salt, pepper and paprika. The sauce should be heavily spiced.

6 Pour the sauce over the salad and mix everything together. Let it stand for about 10 minutes to allow the flavour to go through and then serve.

Crispy Vegetable and Rice Platter

Serves 4

250 ml (9 fl oz) veg-
etable stock
100–150 g (3.5–5 oz)
whole wheat rice
1 cucumber
1 bunch of radishes
3 carrots
4 spring onions
4 tbsp raspberry vine-
gar
salt
lemon pepper
5 tbsp grape seed oil
50 g (2 oz) 8-herbs-
mix from the deep
freezer

Preparation time:
approx. 35 minutes
Per serving:
approx. 346 kcal/1554 kJ
5 g P • 17 g F • 40 g C

1 Bring the vegetable stock to the boil.
Then add the rice and cook at a low
heat for about 20–25 minutes. Wash and
slice the cucumber.

2 Wash the radishes and cut into thin
slices. Take the radish tops and set
them aside as a garnish.

3 Peel and finely grate the carrots.
Wash the spring onions and cut them
into fine rings.

4 To make the marinade, take the vinegar, salt, pepper and oil and mix them
together with the herbs. Mix this together
with the vegetables.

5 Take the mixed vegetables and mix
them together with the rice. Serve lukewarm with the radish greens as a garnish.

Warm Rice Salad

Serves 4

200 g (7 oz)
brown lentils
salt
200 g (7 oz)
Basmati rice
1 bunch of
spring onions
2 cloves of garlic
100 ml (3 fl oz)
olive oil
2 tsp ground
cinnamon
2 tsp paprika
powder
2 tsp ground cumin
black pepper
2 tbsp freshly
chopped coriander

Preparation time:
approx. 50 minutes
(plus soaking time)
Per serving:
approx. 465 kcal/1953 kJ
16 g P • 14 g F • 68 g C

Tip
This salad, served with
fresh bread, is a perfect
starter. It is also a great
main course dish.

1 Soak the lentils overnight in water. On the next day, pour off the water and cook for about 40 minutes in salt water. 20 minutes before it is time to take the beans off the heat, add the rice.

2 Clean the spring onions and cut them into rings. Peel and press the cloves of garlic. Heat the oil in a pan and add the garlic and onion, then sauté for about 5 minutes.

3 Add the herbs to the pan and braise everything for an additional 5 minutes at a low temperature. Wash and shake dry the coriander and then chop.

4 Pour the water off the lentils and rice and put them through a strainer to remove the excess water. Stir in the braised herbs and the chopped coriander. Add salt and pepper to taste. Serve warm.

Green Pasta Salad

1 Bring 3 l (3 qt) of salt water to the boil. Add the pasta and cook according to the instructions on the packet until firm.

2 At the same time bring 2 l (2 qt) of salt water to the boil in a different saucepan. Wash the mange tout and cut off the ends. Blanch the mange tout for a short time in the boiling water. Rinse them with cold water in a colander.

3 Clean the pepper, halve it and remove the seeds. Then cut it into small pieces

4 Wash the spring onions and cut them into small rings. Wash, dry and chop the herbs finely.

5 Pour the water off the noodles and let the excess water drain off in a colander. Mix together the yoghurt, cream and horseradish. Add salt and pepper to taste.

6 Mix the dressing and the vegetables together. Then add the noodles, mix them thoroughly together and serve lukewarm.

Serves 4

salt
**250 g (9 oz) sliced
spaghetti
100 g (3.5 oz)
mange tout
1 red pepper
1 bunch of spring
onions
1/2 bunch of dill
1/2 bunch of basil
1 bunch of Italian
parsley
4 tbsp yoghurt
4 tbsp cream
1 tbsp horseradish
pepper**

Preparation time:
approx. 30 minutes
Per serving:
approx. 255 kcal/1071 kJ
10 g P • 2 g F • 48 g C

Taboulé

Serves 4

200 g (7 oz) bulgur
1 bunch of Italian
parsley
4 sprigs of fresh mint
1/2 cucumber
4 spring onions
2 beef tomatoes
juice from 2 lemons
4 tbsp olive oil
salt
black pepper

Preparation time:
approx. 20 minutes
(plus standing time)
Per serving:
approx. 308 kcal/1291 kJ
6 g P • 13 g F • 42 g C

1 Cook the bulgur in 1/2 l (17 fl oz) of water for about 10 minutes and them take the pot off the stove and let it expand for another 20 minutes.

2 In the meantime wash the parsley and mint. Shake dry and chop.

3 Peel and dice the cucumber. Clean, wash and finely chop the spring onions.

4 Wash the tomatoes and remove the stems. Then dice the flesh.

5 Loosen the bulgur with a fork. Mix with the vegetables and the herbs.

6 Mix together the lemon juice, oil, salt and pepper and pour it over the vegetable salad. Let it stand for at least one hour. Mix one more time, then serve.

Tip
You may substitute bulgur with white semolina if you like. The choice of vegetables can also vary according to your taste.

Potato Salad

1 Wash the potatoes thoroughly and put them in a saucepan full of water. Add the caraway seeds and salt and let everything simmer at a medium heat for about 20 minutes.

2 Wash the radishes, cut off the greens and slice the roots. Mix the mayonnaise with the buttermilk together in a bowl. Add the sugar and lemon juice.

3 Strain the gherkins and corn in a colander. Then cut the gherkins into pieces. Pour the water off the potatoes and let them cool. Slice the potatoes and put them together with the vegetables in a bowl.

4 Fold the finely chopped herbs into the mayonnaise. Then add salt and pepper to taste. Mix the sauce together with the salad and let it stand for about 10 minutes. Arrange on plates and garnish with dill.

Serves 4

400 g (14 oz) pota-
toes
1 tsp caraway seeds
1 tbsp coarse salt
1 bunch of radishes
7 tbsp mayonnaise
250 ml (9 fl oz)
buttermilk
1/2 tsp sugar
1 tbsp lemon juice
2 medium sized
gherkins from the jar
150 g (5 oz) baby
corn from the jar
1/2 bunch of dill
1/2 tsp herbes de
Provence
pepper
dill for garnish

Preparation time:
approx. 40 minutes
Per serving:
approx. 335 kcal/1409 kJ
7 g P • 15 g F • 33 g C

Tip
Potatoes have different qualities for use in the kitchen. The firmer cooking varieties of potatoes are the best for a salad. Ask your greengrocer for advice.

Red Potato Salad

Serves 4

400 g (14 oz)
potatoes
sea salt
1 tbsp caraway
400 g (14 oz) whole
beetroot from the jar
1 bunch of spring
onions
10 sage leaves
1 bunch of radishes
100 g (3.5 oz)
horseradish
200 g (7 oz)
cucumber
200 ml (7 fl oz)
soured milk
1 tbsp paprika
powder
2 tbsp chilli oil
Tabasco sauce
herbs for garnish

Preparation time:
approx. 40 minutes
Per serving:
approx. 238 kcal/1000 kJ
5 g P • 11 g F • 23 g C

1 Wash the potatoes and cook them in their skins for about 15 minutes in sea salt and caraway seeds.

2 Dice the beetroot. Then wash and cut the spring onions and cut them into small rings.

3 Wash and dry the sage and chop it finely. Clean and slice the radishes.

4 Peel the horseradish and the cucumber, then dice. Pour the water off the potatoes and dice.

5 To make the sauce, mix together the soured milk, paprika and chilli oil. Add Tabasco to taste.

6 Put all of the vegetables in a bowl and pour the sauce on top. Let everything stand for about 10 minutes. Then serve garnished with the herbs.

Macaroni Salad

1 Cook the noodles according to the instructions on the packet until they are firm. Then pour off the water, strain and put the noodles back into the saucepan.

2 Peel the fresh asparagus. Wash the pepper, remove its seeds and dice. Peel and finely chop the onion.

3 Cook the asparagus for about 10–12 minutes in an asparagus cooker. Then cut them into slanted bite-sized pieces

4 Cut the salmon into pieces and mix with the other ingredients.

5 Make a creamy sauce in the mixer from the cream cheese, lemon juice and Tabasco. Add the dill last and stir the sauce into the salad. Cover and put in a cool place.

6 Wash the tomatoes and remove the stems. Halve or slice the flesh. Peel the cucumber and cut into sticks. Arrange the salad on plates and garnish with the tomatoes and cucumbers.

Serves 4

150 g (5 oz) macaroni
2 tbsp mayonnaise
250 g (9 oz) asparagus
1 large red pepper
1/2 medium sized onion
200 g (7 oz) cooked salmon
without the skin
1 tbsp Worcester-shire sauce
125 g (5 oz) low fat cream cheese
2 tbsp lemon juice
2–3 dashes of Tabasco sauce
1–2 tbsp chopped dill
15 cherry tomatoes
5 plum tomatoes
1 large cucumber

Preparation time:
approx. 40 minutes
Per serving:
approx. 146 kcal/610 kJ
12 g P • 2 g F • 21 g C

Salads
with Fruits
& Cheeses

Pomegranate and Avocado

Serves 4

3 pomegranates
400 g (14 oz) white
grapes
4 tbsp mint leaves
3 tbsp raspberry
vinegar
2 tbsp olive oil
3 tbsp Grenadine
1 tsp honey
salt
pepper
2 avocados
2 tbsp lemon juice

Preparation time:
approx. 35 minutes
Per serving:
approx. 490 kcal/2060 kJ
10 g P • 14 g F • 8 g C

1 Halve the pomegranates, loosen and remove the stones. Wash the grapes, cut them in half and remove the seeds.

2 Finely chop 2 tbsp mint leaves. Mix them together with the vinegar, oil, Grenadine and honey. Add salt and pepper to taste.

3 Peel the avocados, cut them in half and remove the seeds and slice. Sprinkle them with lemon juice afterwards.

4 Mix together the pomegranate seeds and the grapes in some of the marinade.

5 Place each portion of the salad on the plates and divide the rest of the marinade among the servings. Garnish with mint.

Caribbean Watercress

1 Wash the watercress and field lettuce, dry and tear the leaves. Afterwards soak the raisins in some water.

2 Peel and dice the baby pineapple. Next, peel the orange and the grapefruit so that all white parts are removed. Then loosen and cut out the individual fillets.

3 Dry roast the pine nuts in a pan. Mix all of the ingredients except the pine nuts in a bowl.

4 For the marinade, mix together the pineapple juice and the fruit vinegar. Add salt and pepper to taste. Sprinkle the salad with the dressing and serve garnished with pine nuts.

Serves 4

200 g (7 oz) water-
cress
100 g (3.5 oz) field
lettuce
3 tbsp raisins
1 baby pineapple
1 orange
1 pink grapefruit
3 tbsp pine nuts
4 tbsp pineapple
juice
2 tbsp fruit vinegar
4 tbsp grape seed oil
salt

Preparation time:
approx. 25 minutes
Per serving:
approx. 257 kcal/1076 kJ
4 g P • 16 g F • 22 g C

Chicory Royal

1 Wash and dry the chicory, cut it open lengthways and cut out the core. Cut the leaves into strips. Wash the grapes, cut them in half and remove the pips. Peel the mango, cut it in half and remove the seed. Then slice the mango's flesh. Next halve the melon, remove the seeds and scoop out the flesh with an ice cream scoop.

2 Cut the dates in half, remove the stones and cut into strips. Mix all of the ingredients in a bowl with the buttermilk, grappa, double cream and mango juice. Then spice to taste. Pour the dressing over the salad. Garnish with pecans and flower blossoms.

Serves 4

2 heads of chicory
400 g (14 oz) grapes
1 mango
1/2 honeydew
melon
100 g (3.5 oz) dried
dates
250 ml (9 oz)
buttermilk
5 tbsp grappa
2 tbsp double cream
3 tbsp mango juice
lemon pepper
cardamom and
powdered cloves
50 g (2 oz) chopped
pecans
flowers for garnish

Preparation time:
approx. 30 minutes
Per serving:
approx. 261 kcal/1097 kJ
6 g P • 14 g F • 20 g C

Gourmet Avocado Salad

Serves 4

**200 g (7 oz)
blackberries
3 avocados
2 tbsp lemon juice
200 g (7 oz)
mushrooms
2 tbsp butter
salt
2 tbsp lemon pepper
150 g (5 oz) cherry
tomatoes
4 tbsp grapefruit
juice
3 tbsp banana juice
3 tbsp Grenadine
3 puréed kiwis
6 tbsp pumpkin
seed oil
125 ml (4 fl oz)
vegetable broth
pepper
kiwi for garnish**

Preparation time:
approx. 35 minutes
Per serving:
approx. 590 kcal/2306 kJ
9 g P • 29 g F • 13 g C

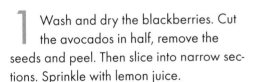

1 Wash and dry the blackberries. Cut the avocados in half, remove the seeds and peel. Then slice into narrow sections. Sprinkle with lemon juice.

2 Wash the mushrooms and cut them in half. Heat the butter in a pan and sauté the mushrooms in it. Season them with salt and lemon pepper.

3 Wash the tomatoes, cut them in half and add them to the mushrooms, cooking them for about 3 minutes. Take the vegetables out of the pan and let them cool.

4 Mix the blackberries and the avocado slices together. Then to make the dressing, mix together the different juices

and then add the kiwi purée and pumpkin seed oil. Add salt and pepper to taste.

5 Pour the dressing over the salad, garnish with kiwi slices and serve.

Tip

Guacamole, a Mexican dip made from avocados, is very simple to make and it does not require much extra effort. Simply take some mashed avocados and add some chopped and peeled tomatoes, fresh onions, herbs, salt, garlic and a little lime juice. This very well known Mexican dip is ideal for seafood, salads and tortillas

149

Fruit with Gorgonzola

Serves 4

1 large butterhead
lettuce
1 small pear
75 g (2.5 oz)
strawberries
1/2 onion
3 tbsp sherry or
apple juice
2 tbsp balsamic vine-
gar
1 tbsp sugar
1 tsp sunflower seed
oil
15 g (0.5 oz)
Gorgonzola

Preparation time:
approx. 15 minutes
Per serving:
approx. 55 kcal/230 kJ
2 g P • 2 g F • 9 g C

1 Wash and shake dry the lettuce and tear into bite-sized pieces. Peel the pear, take out the core and cut into thin slices. Wash the strawberries and let them dry. Peel the onion and cut it into rings.

2 Mix together the lettuce, fruit and onions in a bowl.

3 Stir together the sherry (or apple juice), vinegar, sugar and oil until the sugar is dissolved.

4 Pour the dressing over the salad and mix together thoroughly. Serve sprinkled with crumbled cheese.

Onion Salad with Roquefort

1 Peel the oranges so that there is no white skin left on the fruit. Then remove the fillets by taking a sharp knife and separating each fillet on the cleavage between each slice. Next, wash and quarter the apple, remove the core and slice thinly. Then mix with the orange fillets immediately.

2 Tear off the lettuce leaves and wash them, then shake them dry. Clean and wash the spring onions and cut them into thin rings.

3 Mash the Roquefort and mix in with the yoghurt. Then stir in the port wine and vinegar. Add salt and pepper to taste.

4 Divide the lettuce leaves on the plates. Then place the onions and fruit on top. Finally pour the sauce on top of the salad.

Serves 4

2 oranges
1 apple
1 lollo rosso
300 g (10 oz) spring
onions
50 g (2 oz)
Roquefort
80 g (3 oz) yoghurt
2 tbsp port wine
2 tbsp herb vinegar
salt
freshly ground
white pepper

Preparation time:
approx. 25 minutes
Per serving:
approx. 194 kcal/816 kJ
6 g P • 8 g F • 18 g C

Mango Kiwi Salad

Serves 4

1 mango
3 kiwis
200 g (7 oz) blue
cheese
1 lollo rosso
2 tbsp lemon juice
salt
pepper from the mill
sugar
4 tbsp oil
lemon balm for
garnish

Preparation time:
approx. 20 minutes
Per serving:
approx. 363 kcal/1525 kJ
11 g P • 27 g F • 11 g C

1 Peel the mango and slice its flesh from the stone. Then slice it again into bite-sized pieces.

2 Peel the kiwi, halve it lengthways and then slice.

3 Dice the cheese. Then wash and shake dry the lettuce and tear it into bite-sized pieces.

4 Mix the lemon juice with salt, pepper and sugar. Then beat in the oil.

5 Mix all of the salad ingredients together with the dressing. Garnish with lemon balm and serve.

Orange Salad

Serves 4

4 oranges
6 dried figs
1 tsp orange blos-
som water
1 tsp sugar
1/2 tsp cinnamon
75 g (2.5 oz) sliced
almonds
some mint leaves

Preparation time:
approx. 15 minutes
(plus standing time)
Per serving:
approx. 325 kcal/1365 kJ
8 g P • 12 g F • 45 g C

1 Peel the oranges and remove the white parts of the rind from the flesh. Then cut the orange diagonally into slices. Then cut the figs into thin strips.

2 Combine the orange slices and figs in a bowl. Sprinkle them with orange blossom water, sugar and cinnamon.

3 Let the salad stand for 30 minutes, then stir in the almonds

4 Serve garnished with mint. This dish goes well as a dessert or as an accompaniment to chicken dishes.

Fruit Salad

Serves 4

1 orange (125 g/
5 oz of actual
orange flesh)
300 g (10 oz) white
and blue grapes
1 sour and juicy
apple 150 g (5 oz),
e.g. Granny Smith
1 juicy pear
(125 g/5 oz)
2 tbsp chopped
almonds
1 tbsp maple syrup
100 g (3.5 oz) whole
milk yoghurt

Preparation time:
approx. 10 minutes
Per serving:
approx. 160 kcal/671 kJ
3 g P • 4 g F • 27 g C

1 Peel the oranges and remove all of the white from the rind. Then separate the fruit into slices and cut into bite-sized pieces.

2 Wash the grapes under running water, tear off the grapes from the vine, halve and remove the pips.

3 Wash the apple and the pear. Quarter each and remove the core, then cut into small slices.

4 Put all of the fruit into a large bowl and mix. Then, divide among 4 small bowls and sprinkle 2 tbsp of almonds on top for each portion.

5 Mix the yoghurt and maple syrup together. Pour the sauce over each portion of the salad and serve.

Melon with Vinaigrette

1 Remove the seeds from the melon and take out the flesh with an ice cream scoop. Peel the cucumber and cut it into small cubes. Pour hot water over the tomatoes and remove their skins. Then take out the seeds and dice.

2 Take the melon, cucumber and diced tomatoes and combine them in a bowl. Then add some salt and 2 tbsp of mint and mix. Let the ingredients stand for a few minutes.

3 In the meantime make a vinaigrette from the oil, vinegar, the rest of the mint, cumin and salt. Pour it over the salad and let it stand for another 30 minutes.

4 Arrange the melon salad the way you like and add mint as a garnish.

Serves 4

1/2 cantaloupe melon
1/2 cucumber
3 tomatoes
salt
3 tbsp freshly chopped mint
3 tbsp olive oil
2 tbsp white balsamic vinegar
1/2 tsp ground cumin
mint for garnish

Preparation time:
approx. 15 minutes
(plus standing time)
Per serving:
approx. 102 kcal/426 kJ
1 g P • 9 g F • 3 g C

Fig Cocktail

1 Wash, peel and slice the figs. Put all of it into a mould and sprinkle with Grand Marnier and lemon juice.

2 Wash and dry the lemon balm, cut it into strips and sprinkle on top of the figs. Let everything stand for about 5 minutes.

3 Cut the beef prosciutto into paper thin slices.

4 Roll up the meat and place it on the plates. Arrange the lettuce in a decorative manner and lay the figs on top. Serve with grissini.

Serves 4

500 g (17 oz) figs
2 cl (3 oz) Grand
Marnier
1 tbsp lemon juice
1 bunch lemon balm
100 g (3.5 oz) air-
dried beef ham
lettuce leaves for
garnish (e.g. lollo
rosso or field lettuce)
4 grissini (Italian
style bread sticks)

Preparation time:
approx. 10 minutes
Per serving:
approx. 147 kcal/620 kJ
7 g P • 2 g F • 22 g C

Stuffed Melon

Serves 4

2 honeydew melons
200 g (7 oz) cherries
200 g (7 oz) straw-
berries
1 peach
1–2 kiwis
200 g (7 oz)
pineapple
5 tbsp Grand
Marnier
125 g (5 oz) sugar

Preparation time:
approx. 20 minutes
(plus cooling time)
Per serving:
approx. 328 kcal/1378 kJ
2 g P • 1 g F • 33 g C

1 Cut the melons in half and remove the seeds. Take the fruit out up until about 1 cm (0.2 in) before the rind.

2 Cool the melon halves. Then wash the strawberries and the cherries, remove the stems and remove the stones from the cherries. Cut the cherries and strawberries in half, then peel the rest of the fruit and cut into small pieces.

3 Mix together the Grand Marnier and sugar. Add the fruit and chill for about 30 minutes. Then fill the melon halves and serve.

Berries with a White Sauce

Serves 4

300 g (10 oz) seed-
less wine grapes
300 g (10 oz) black-
berries (fresh or
frozen)
150 g (5 oz) low fat
milk curds
150 g (5 oz) natural
yoghurt
150 ml (5 fl oz) milk
50 ml (2 fl oz) cream
some sugar and
cinnamon
2 tbsp pistachios

Preparation time:
approx. 20 minutes
Per serving:
approx. 211 kcal/887 kJ
8 g P • 14 g F • 18 g C

1 Wash and dry the grapes. Then clean the blackberries and after drying them mix them in with the grapes. Mix them together thoroughly. If the blackberries are frozen, then they should be allowed to thaw first.

2 Mix the curds with the yoghurt and milk. Stir until it is smooth. Whip the cream until stiff, then fold it into the curd and yoghurt mixture.

3 Sweeten and spice the curd and yoghurt mixture to taste with sugar and cinnamon.

4 Chop the pistachios into small pieces and add about 1 tsp to the mixed berries. Stir. Then sprinkle the rest on top as garnish. Serve the salad with the sauce on the side.

Fruit Royal

1 Mash up the Gorgonzola cheese with a fork. Then add the cream and stir together thoroughly until it is very creamy. At some point you may need to add a little bit more cream or some milk.

2 Put the cream mixture into an icing bag with a large star icing tip on the end. Then place it in the refrigerator.

3 Chop the nuts and dry roast them in a pan on top of the stove for about 4 minutes until they are golden brown, then set them on the side.

4 Wash and dry the plums and remove the stones. Wash and peel the pears. Cut the pears into quarters and remove the cores. Slice both the pears and the plums. Place the fruit onto 4 large plates in a decorative fashion.

5 Cover the plate with the white sauce, pressing it from the icing bag. Sprinkle the salad with walnut and powder everything with cinnamon.

Serves 4

200 g (7 oz) Gorgonzola
6–7 tbsp cream and a little milk to taste
4 tbsp walnuts
400 g (14 oz) plums
200 g (7 oz) pears
cinnamon

Preparation time:
approx. 25 minutes
Per serving:
approx. 365 kcal/1533 kJ
12 g P • 12 g F • 14 g C

Index of Recipes